The Emotion Driven Life

Dr. Bill Purvis

Table of Contents

དཀ

Introduction

Every person is driven by something. What drives your life? Is it money? Power? Popularity? Ambition? Validation? Acceptance? Something else? Pastor Rick Warren's bestseller, *The Purpose Driven Life,* encouraged millions of readers to live their lives with God's purpose in mind. It is a book that focused on how our Creator designed us to live our lives. If you haven't read it you really should, it's a great book! However, as a pastor for over thirty years I've discovered that most people miss the point. I believe that most people are letting the "Emotion Driven Life" guide them. Think about it—emotions like lust, bitterness, anger, guilt, and fear direct a lot of our choices.

Emotions are fluid, always flowing. If your life is driven by ever-changing emotions, then you'll never be able to direct your destiny. I know a guy who is terrified of flying.

He lives in South Georgia and believes that if he can't drive to a place, then it's not worth seeing. Of all things, Mr. Fearful won an all-expenses paid trip to Hawaii. What does he do? Since he's driven by fear, he passes on the trip of a lifetime. Emotion driven people always miss out on the best experiences. This is not God's will for us. God didn't create you to be imprisoned by your emotions. In this book, we are going to explore emotions that can rob you of your potential and help you get control of them, so that you can reach your destiny. I believe that the "truths" of these biblical insights will give you a newfound freedom of release and victory. It's time for you to conquer the Emotion Driven Life!

Chapter One

The Javelin of Jealousy

Saul's Green-Eyed Monster

My best friend's dad, who happens to be my employer, hates me. I don't know where it came from. One minute, I'm his favorite go-to guy; the next, I'm on his hit list. I mean, I go toe-to-toe with this guy's worst enemies, even battling it out with some enormous freak show that everyone else is too scared to touch. And he still can't stand me! Come on, where's the love? As if things weren't messed up enough already, you should have seen what he did yesterday! I'm just relaxing, playing a little music, when out of nowhere, a spear comes flying by my head. I look up, and my best friend's dad is glaring at me. He's not mad because of the tunes I was playing, but because his spear didn't pin me to the wall. What in the world did I ever do to that guy?

This may not be exactly what David was thinking, but I bet I'm not far off. First Samuel 18:6-12 gives us our first glimpse of Saul's jealousy of David. David is a shepherd, the youngest and smallest of his brothers, and Saul is a great and powerful king. David has saved his nation by killing the giant Goliath, but he has no idea he is going to meet an even bigger giant. A giant called "jealousy." David is moving up the ranks in Saul's army, and it appears that everyone is pleased with him. That is, everyone but Saul.

Jealousy first rears its ugly head in Saul's life when he hears women in the street dancing and singing, ". . . Saul has killed his thousands, and David his ten thousands!" (1 Sam. 18:7 NLT). Suddenly, Saul is stopped in his tracks. "Whoa, wait a minute," he wonders. "Do they think David is better than me? He's only killed one giant, but I've been their faithful king all these years, making sure they're safe at night. If they're already singing songs about him, he may decide to take my kingdom from me!" (1 Sam. 18:8). From that point on, anytime Saul hears anyone mention David's name, his ears perk up.

Saul can't get the women's song out of his head and goes irate every time he thinks about David. This leads to his attempt on David's life. David dodges the spear once, but Saul doesn't let that keep him from trying again later. Saul is so jealous of David that he can't think about anything else. His obsession with David reaches the boiling point and he grabs a javelin and hurls it at David-twice! My friend Gary Levi is a missionary in a very dark region. He once gave me a javelin from a tribe that had been used to take many lives.

Believe me, the real javelins like this and the one hurled at David were meant to cause harm.

Jealousy is a sin that robs your joy. If you allow it in, it will take over and make you miserable! We often confuse jealousy with envy, but they are not the same. Envy means you want what somebody else has. For example, maybe your neighbor just bought a new boat, and every time you see it you wish it were yours. Jealousy means you want them not to have it. Jealousy takes offense and is threatened by another's success or progress.

You've seen it . . . That friend who always buys the same shirt you just wore, picks up every new hobby you try out, and always plans the same trips you take. Jealous people don't have to think; they just copy what you do. Jealous people don't want you to have anything. They are threatened by your success and can't handle it. They don't want you to have your fifteen minutes in the sun. I give credit to Dr. Charles Stanley for first making me aware of the common six objects of jealousy. As I've observed through the years these areas really do have an influence in people's lives.

These areas of jealousy are:

1. People
2. Possessions
3. Position
4. Privileges
5. Personality
6. Popularity

People—People often are the object of our jealousy. Tabloid magazines are so popular because of our curiosity about other people's lives. For three dollars and fifty cents, you can get a glimpse of other people's dirt. Jealousy sells these magazines to unfulfilled people, hoping to get satisfaction from seeing someone else's flaws.

Possessions—Another common object of jealousy is possessions. We're concerned about what others have. If someone buys a new car, then some people become suspicious that they must be selling drugs or stealing from their boss. If a neighbor moves up into a better neighborhood and a larger house, then they surely must be doing something crooked or have inherited some money they didn't earn. A jealous person cannot accept the fact that if others advance, perhaps it simply is because they have worked hard and God has blessed them.

Position—Position also can be an object of jealousy. A person who is jealous of another's position may ask, "How did she get that job? She must have known somebody on the inside. She must have kissed up to the right person, or mingled with the right crowd."

Privileges—The fourth object of jealousy is privilege. We think, "Well, they've got it made. They live a life of ease and don't have any problems. They were given all they have and are above 'real life.'" I love that song lyric, "I got problems, you got problems, all God's children have problems." We all have problems in different forms; some people just handle their problems differently.

Personality—Another object of jealousy is personality. Some people light up a room when they walk in it . . . and others don't. There's nothing wrong with either one. This type of jealousy says, "He's so well-liked, all eyes are on him. I despise the attention he receives."

Popularity—A person's popularity is another object of our jealousy. Some people live to be popular and are jealous when someone else is better known or respected. Jealous people feel threatened that others are "stealing" their light.

This is the type of jealousy Saul had for David. David killed a giant and became popular overnight—Saul hated him for it.

". . . Who Can Stand Before Jealousy?" (Proverbs 27:4)

Jealousy stems from one thing . . . *insecurity*. You see, although David's popularity is the object of Saul's jealousy, Saul's hidden insecurity causes the jealousy in the first place. He is insecure that this young guy is getting too much credit. The women in the street praising David may have exaggerated his success, but that does not make Saul feel any better. Instead of rejoicing with others and letting David have his day in the sun, Saul is offended. "*. . . They have ascribed to David ten thousands, but to me they have ascribed thousands*" (1 Sam. 18:8). Saul's insecurity is surfacing.

We need to ask ourselves from time to time, "Can I handle the praise of another? Can I handle the success of others?" Don't allow your insecurity to feed jealousy in your life.

Jealousy causes chaos, and its consequences are devastating. You can't have a relationship with a jealous person, because jealousy always destroys. James 3:16 describes the fruit of jealousy: "*For where jealousy and selfish ambition exist, there is disorder and every evil thing.*" Jealous people make life way too complicated. I had to break a relationship with a jealous person once, because he was always reading into every little thing that I or anyone else did. He reminded me of the two psychiatrists that were passing each other on the street. One said, "Good morning," and the other thought to himself, "I wonder what he meant by that?" Jealous people just can't keep things simple.

Proverbs 27:4 says, *"Wrath is fierce and anger is a flood, but who can stand before jealousy?"* This verse says it perfectly: wrath and anger are both really bad, but neither is as devastating as jealousy. Jealousy always destroys. Kudzu grows all over the South. This plant is wild! It's an unmanageable weed; once it starts growing, it takes over everything in the yard: your house, your car . . . even your dog better watch out! Jealousy is like kudzu because once it enters your life, it destroys everything in its path.

Jealousy clouds your reasoning, poisons your heart, blinds your eyes, and makes you believe outrageous lies. The hate of a jealous person turns all those who disagree into enemies. It can tear apart families.

A sweet woman in our church was telling me recently about a sad situation within her own family. This lady's mother is very jealous, and therefore suspicious, of a well-respected businessman in our town. Bringing this man down seems to be her goal. The thing is, her daughter does a lot of business with the man and is a friend of his. She has asked her mother several times to please leave the man alone, not only because her accusations are completely false and slanderous, but also because it is starting to affect her daughter's business. And do you know what the woman told her daughter? She said, "Well, if you don't like my opinion of him, then you can find somewhere else to go at Christmas. You're not welcome in my home!" Can you believe that? Turning her back on her own daughter? Saul lashes out at his son Jonathan because he defends David (1 Sam. 20).

A jealous person doesn't want to see the best in others, rather accusing every action and distorting every motive. Saul allows jealousy to grow in his life until he is boiling over (1 Sam. 18:8). He should have been the first to congratulate David. He should have been rushing to high-five David and invite him over for a rack of lambs. Instead, he lets jealousy blind his eyes and grow into hatred.

First Samuel 18:9 tells us that *"Saul looked at David with suspicion from that day on."* Saul is obsessed with David. He's like a creepy stalker, thinking about him all day long and twisting his words at every opportunity. Saul is so determined to destroy David that he can't even enjoy his own life or kingdom. The guy has lost it! He's a king and lives in a palace. He has everything to enjoy. He could have found a million other things to occupy his time, but he allowed jealousy to blur his reasoning.

Saul's jealousy is so out of control that he doesn't throw a spear at only David. He throws one at Jonathan, his own son, just for being friends with him! He's obsessed with jealousy and hates anyone who supports David, even his own flesh (1 Sam. 20:32-33).

Here's the deal . . . You'll either conquer jealousy or it will conquer you; and if it conquers you, it will rob you of all your peace. Jealous people may keep it hidden initially. David never sees it coming. He thinks Saul loves and respects him; but then, out of nowhere, comes a javelin. Perhaps you've experienced a Saul in your life. You got a new position at work, a new car, that dream home you've always wanted. Rather than hearing compliments, you get criticism. Jealous people really have a gift for taking the wind out of your sails. Remember that friends celebrate wins.

Think about the lives in the Bible that were damaged by jealousy. Jealousy causes the first murder in the Bible, when Cain kills his brother Abel. Jealousy causes Joseph's brothers to sell him into slavery. His dad had given him a new coat, and they couldn't take it. Why didn't they just say, "Hey, little brother, cool threads"? Their jealousy would not allow it. Jealousy will not allow you to rejoice in the successes of others. Jesus teaches us how the prodigal son returning home to his father, after squandering his inheritance, is faced with his jealous older brother. Big bro was mad that his little brother had run off and went partying, but then still gets his father's blessing when he returns home. Jealousy even played a big role in Jesus' crucifixion. When he turns Jesus over to be crucified, Pontius Pilate says, *"For he knew that because of envy they had handed Him over"* (Matt. 27:18).

Jealousy develops when we compare ourselves to others. It festers when we start to compare our house to their house, our car to their car, our money to their money, and so on. It can make you think less of yourself. I heard about a guy who was so jealous of his coworker that he couldn't stand him. One night, God woke him up from his sleep. God said to the jealous guy, "Look, I will give you anything you want. All you have to do is ask. The only catch is that whatever you ask for, I'm going to give double to your coworker. For example, if you ask for a new car, then your coworker is going to get two new cars. If you ask for a new house, he's going to get two new houses . . . got it?" The guy thought about it for a while and then suddenly he said, "I got it! God, I want to be blind in one eye!" That's jealousy! It's amazing how insecurity can grow into full-blown jealousy. Saul kept himself from receiving God's best blessings because jealousy took over his life.

Get Rid of It!!

Saul never was able to conquer jealousy. In fact, I don't know of a single person in the Bible that did. However, just because he couldn't doesn't mean you can't. You see, we need to rid ourselves of jealousy because it prevents God from blessing us. God wants to bless you. However, He can't do that if jealousy is in your heart. If you're focused on another's blessings, you can't focus on your own. He wants your complete attention on the gifts He's given *you,* not the ones He has given to someone else. There are three things you can today to help you conquer jealousy. No, it may not happen overnight, but if you'll consistently put these steps into action, you eventually can stop jealousy dead in its tracks.

First, you've got to **admit it.** We never like admitting our flaws, do we? We have this idea that admitting we are wrong will make us look weak. But I want you to trust me. Just like admitting to your sin to God brings freedom, so also admitting your jealousy will bring release from it. It goes something like this: "My name is Tom and I'm jealous of Steve because . . ." You've got to tell God, "I have messed up. I resent what he has, and I want to be free of this jealousy."

The next step is to **stop thinking about the object of your jealousy.** New Yorkers often say . . . "Forget about it!" That could not be better advice! Just forget about it! Have you ever heard the saying, "He who angers you controls you"? The same principle applies to jealousy. If all you can think about is the object of your jealousy, then you will remain hindered by it. Do yourself a favor and forget about it! Keep it out of your mind.

Finally, **reflect on your blessings and be content.** Instead of focusing on what you think you're missing, focus on what you already have. You're alive. Start with that and then see what else you can come up with. It's amazing how many blessings we find in our own lives when we take a minute to look. Learn to celebrate your blessings with God.

If you train yourself to focus on all of the blessings God has given you, large and small, you will realize that there is no reason to be jealous of anyone or anything else!

****

Now, I realize some of you are thinking, "But, Bill, you don't understand! Jealousy isn't something I struggle with. I'm trying to deal with a person who has focused their jealousy toward me—what can I do about that?" I understand how you feel. For those of you who find yourselves the object of someone else's jealousy, here is a checklist for making a clean break.

1. Avoid that person. If you remember, even David had to flee Saul's presence. You need to avoid that jealous individual at all costs. This may mean ending a friendship. It might mean distancing yourself from a certain family member. Sometimes, because of the negative influence certain people have in our life, we simply may have to love them from afar. It is not always the easiest thing to do, but it will be much better for your life in the long run.

2. Don't waste time and energy responding. Your jealous critics will hate this, but remember it says in Proverbs that you can't change a fool (Proverbs 23:9). I've noticed in my life that whenever I respond to negativity, the situation usually gets worse, not better. Life is way too precious to waste time on ignorance.

3. Understand that people will forgive you for anything but success.

Think about it . . . if David had just delivered the bread and cheese and not killed the giant (1 Sam. 17:18), then there never would have been any women singing his praises at all. Saul never would have been jealous, and David never would have been king. Look at Jesus. He could have avoided the cross if He would have kept things status quo with the religious crowd. He would not have been crucified, and we would not have a Savior.

If you will practice these steps, you will be able to keep your life moving forward, no longer allowing your critics to stall you. I hope that whether you're a victim of jealousy or someone struggling with this emotion, you will apply everything we've talked about in this chapter. You only have one life to live, so don't waste it. The cure for jealousy is becoming more obsessed with Jesus than we are with others.

Chapter Two

The Bondage of Bitterness

What's in a Name?

W as I not good enough? My whole life, I always have tried to do the right thing. And for what? So that I could end up widowed by the only man I'd ever loved? My heart aches from morning to night with no end in sight. How could God do this to me? You would think He'd punish the rebellious and the hypocrites, not his faithful servants. Instead, I'm now left to wander this earth alone and miserable. And there she sits . . . a constant reminder of how perfect my life used to be. I told her to get out of here, but she's more stubborn than any woman I've ever met. She's followed my every move—even all the way back here to Bethlehem. I guess I should be grateful, but I can't find it in me.

This may describe how Naomi felt after losing her husband and sons. Naomi had married Elimelech (or Eli for short). Naomi and her family had set out for Moab to escape a famine in Bethlehem. Once there, Naomi's two sons marry Moabite women. Just when things were looking good for this family, tragedy strikes and Eli dies. Naomi is heartbroken. I know those of you who have lost a spouse can relate. Ten years later, both of Naomi's sons die as well. Now she's left in a foreign land with no surviving blood relatives and two grieving daughters-in-law.

She decides to go back home to Bethlehem and tells her daughters-in-law that they should stay with their families and their land. She wants them to be able to move on with their lives. One of her son's wives, Orpah, agrees and goes back home to her family. Ruth, however, isn't going anywhere. She refuses to leave Naomi's side and travels with her back to Bethlehem. When the two women arrive, they hear people asking, "Is that Naomi?" Naomi hears and tells them not to call her Naomi anymore, but Mara, because the Lord has dealt bitterly with her (Ruth 1:1-22).

Does that story sound familiar to you? Have you ever known anybody with big dreams and big plans, who left town and set out to conquer the world? We want the best for those people, don't we? We want them to succeed. If they don't, it can be disappointing both for them as well as the supporters they left behind. Naomi had left her home many years before, on top of the world, with a great husband and two strong sons. When she comes back many years later, she has no one except a tagalong daughter-in-law. Can you imagine the emptiness, embarrassment, shame, and the complete devastation she must have felt?

Naomi had lived a life of luxury. She had a great husband, two sons, and two wonderful daughters-in-law. But, as happens to many of us, tragedy interrupted her life. Things are going great and then—BAM—something happens that changes everything. Naomi allowed these circumstances to make her bitter. How do you respond when plans go astray or you're faced with a major hit? When treated unfairly, what do you do? Notice I said *when,* not if. Things will happen in your life that you will not like . . . it's a guarantee. It is how you handle yourself during those times that is so important.

Where on Earth Did This Bitter Taste Come From?

Bitterness can come over you quickly. This emotion will smoothly and secretly slide its way in if you're not careful. A deep loss, or any kind of loss, can cause bitterness. You may lose your job, your mate, or even a friend. That's what is so sneaky about bitterness. It slips in whenever your spirit is broken, when you are weak and defenseless. Take a look at Naomi—bitterness leaked in when she lost the most significant men in her life. Bitterness changed her point of view. When we get bitter, our perspective changes as well.

Naomi's **view of her life** changed. Look at the first thing she says to the women in her hometown when she returns: *"I went out full, but the LORD has brought me back empty . . ."* (Ruth 1:21). She's totally drowning in bitterness. She doesn't have the positive outlook she once had, but views her glass as "half empty."

Several years ago, my friend's wife passed away. He was completely devastated and heartbroken, just as anyone would be. He was driving home from the funeral, lost in his thoughts and mourning the loss of his best friend, when he stopped at a red light. He turned his head and saw a couple sitting happily together in the car next to him. They were laughing, singing along to the radio, basically just enjoying life and minding their own business. They had no idea what my friend was going through in the car next to them. Their happiness was more than my poor friend could take. He jumped out of the car and began to bang on the couple's window, shouting, "Don't you know my wife just died?! She died!! How can you be laughing at a time like this?" Obviously, he was suffering a huge hurt. His spirit was broken and he was very weak emotionally. If we're not careful, this is when bitterness can jump right into our lives.

Naomi's **view of herself** also changed. Remember when the hometown girls were asking one another if Naomi was indeed back in town? Instead of saying, "Yeah, it's me," she tells them, "Don't call me Naomi anymore; call me Mara," which means bitter (Ruth 1:20). She no longer wants to be tied to a name that reflects all the good she had in her life. Naomi means "delightsome," and she does not want people to think of that when they think of her. Talk about being down in the dumps! Think of Winnie the Pooh's gloomy friend Eeyore. Naomi becomes like Eeyore. "Whoa is me, life stinks. I'm going to change my name." Her view of herself has changed, and she takes drastic measures to make sure the world views her the same way she views herself.

Naomi's **view of God** changed as well. She says, *". . . the LORD has witnessed against me and the Almighty has afflicted me"* (Ruth 1:21). Naomi feels like God has wronged her. She thinks, "I had everything I ever wanted in life, but God snatched it away from me!" Sometimes it is easy to let God take the blame for the wrong that happens in our lives. In our humanness, we can't understand why something terrible would happen to us. Blaming someone else, even God, makes us feel better.

Remember, <u>**it's easy to be bitter when you've suffered a loss.**</u> While the pain you feel is real and legitimate, you can't allow yourself to focus on it. If you do, it will suck the joy out of your life.

Taking up an offense is another way bitterness can slip into your life. Have you ever taken up an offense for someone? Some of you know what I'm talking about. Maybe your friend got into a disagreement with a mutual acquaintance, and now you give that person the cold shoulder whenever you see him. You're showing him where you stand, whose side you're on. Did you know that God can't bless you if you get involved in someone else's disagreement? God doesn't call us to take sides; He calls us to make peace.

One night, President John F. Kennedy was frustrated, blowing off steam to his wife Jacqueline about how angry he was with a particular senator. Trying to show her loyalty, Jackie completely snubbed the senator when she saw him the next day. A few hours later, she was waiting outside her husband's office to meet him for dinner. To her surprise, JFK and the senator she had snubbed a few hours earlier came out of the office laughing, with their arms around each other. She told JFK later, "I'm so mad at you! Yesterday you told me how angry you were with him, so I spent all night hating him. I even gave him the cold shoulder today, and then you two come out here looking like best friends." (Adapted from *The Eloquent Jacqueline Kennedy Onassis: A Portrait in Her Own Words*. Adler, Bill. p.57)

She had taken up an offense for her husband, but he had resolved the issue. Things were fine between the president and senator, but the First Lady came out bitter. You see, God can give two people who get in a disagreement with one another the grace to handle it and restore the relationship. But God can't give that same kind of grace to a third party.

Putting yourself in the middle of someone else's business always leaves you looking bitter, and it's just not worth it.

Bitterness also develops when you disappoint yourself. After denying Jesus three times, the Bible says that *". . . [Peter] wept bitterly"* (Luke 22:62). Peter's betrayal of Jesus causes a deep wound of self-disappointment. When Jesus had been resurrected, He says, "Go tell the disciples *and Peter* I want to see them" (Mark 16:7). Jesus adds *"and Peter"* because He knows that if He doesn't specifically single Peter out, his friend's shame will keep him away.

Sometimes we can be our own worst critic, beating ourselves up over an out-of-character behavior. Some people hold themselves to a very high moral standard, which is great. However, if they ever miss a step and fall, then they may dwell on feelings of shame and bitterness.

There is a wonderful lady in our church. Although she is a godly woman, she made a mistake many years ago and had an affair. She was in an extremely vulnerable place in her life, and a coworker took advantage of her. Even though this was a one-time failing that went against her nature, she couldn't forgive herself. Her husband had forgiven her and moved past it, but she was too steeped in bitterness to move forward. She once told me, "I wish he would just hate me and divorce me; I don't deserve for him to stay with me." Don't ever let that kind of bitterness take over in your life. Jesus didn't come to save the perfect; He came to save the sinners. He expects you to make mistakes. If He can forgive you, why on earth shouldn't you forgive yourself?

The Cost of Bitterness

The devil can't steal your salvation, but he can steal your joy. He can make you a completely miserable, bitter Christian.

Hebrews 12:15 says, *"See to it that no one falls short of the grace of God and that no bitter root grows up to cause trouble and defile many."* In other words, you can't control the pain, the suffering, or the hurt in your life. However, you can control whether you let that wound make you bitter or better. The choice is up to you. Here's the deal: **The devil tells you that the legitimate wrong done to you justifies your bitterness.** Satan tells you that you're entitled to be bitter because you lost your job or your spouse. And you know what? Sometimes, when the hurt we are experiencing is a legitimate wrong, it's really easy for us to believe that he has a point.

There are so many wonderful people and families in our church who have good cause to be bitter. Week after week, I visit with widows who have lost the love of their lives, parents who have had to bury their children, and brothers and sisters who still can't understand what caused their sibling to take their own life. Bitterness would be an easy choice in any of these situations. But if you allow bitterness to come into your life, then things are only going to go downhill more quickly. It's much harder to climb back up that hill after you've reached the bottom.

Bitterness will cut you off from God's favor, which is His grace. God wants to give you the grace to get you past whatever situation you're going through. But if you're bitter, you'll nurse it, rehearse it, and replay it over and over again. People who used to be your friends will begin to run the other way when they see you coming. Bitterness pushes people away and sucks all the energy and happiness out of the room. Life is too short to carry that problem.

Unchecked bitterness shows up in your attitude and can affect your health, aggravating preexisting conditions. Doctors could prescribe less medication if some of their patients would just learn to forgive. Getting rid of bitterness could cure their sleeplessness and high blood pressure. Imagine your doctor writing, "Forgive these three people," on his slip of paper rather than a prescription for sleeping pills, blood pressure meds, anti-depressants, or anti-anxiety pills. You'd be surprised how well that would work!

Bitterness will draw bitter people to you and push healthy people away from you. The Institute of Basic Youth Conflicts, according to a story told by Bill Gothard, put two rebellious, bitter people in the same room with a couple hundred other students. The two bitter people entered through separate doors, but within seven minutes they found each other! Their common bond of rebellion and bitterness drew them together. Our spirit draws us to similar people. You attract what you are. Take a look at your life: whom do you attract? Do you attract happy, positive people or negative, angry people?

Bitterness pollutes everything and everyone it touches. The Bible says it *"defile[s] many"* (Heb. 12:15). Bitterness wants revenge and holds grudges. You've probably heard someone say, "I don't get mad; I get even." Maybe your husband left you for that cute blonde, and they just went on a cruise together. I bet you want their ship to sink! That'll show 'em.

Have you ever gotten revenge, only to realize it wasn't worth it? Jack Hyles wrote this poem on revenge in his book *Reason With Rhyme:*

I know the empty victor's guilt
When kneeling o'er my fallen prey.
I've held the sword when blood was spilt,
While joys of winning fled away.

He knows what it is like to have gotten revenge and later found out it wasn't all that sweet. Bitterness is like a backpack. When you go to the grocery store, it goes with you. When you go to work, it goes with you. When you go on vacation, it goes with you. Now, you know your bitterness doesn't deserve to go on vacation with you; but if it's in your heart, you're allowing it to come along and enjoy the scenery and good food with you! There is a freedom that comes with releasing your bitterness. Don't allow it to cling onto your life.

Getting Better, Not Bitter

If you really want bitterness removed from your life, then you have got to confess it. Tell God that you're hurt. Ask Him to help you not become bitter. I dealt with bitterness about two years ago. Some people in my life turned against me. I didn't see it coming. I thought, "After all I did to help you, out of the purest of heart, I can't believe this is what I get in return." About every three months, the seed of bitterness would come up, but I would just push it aside. I realized, however, that I could either dwell on it and let it steal my joy or learn from it and move on. I chose the latter and didn't allow the bitterness to take root.

If you are dealing with bitterness toward someone, you have to forgive them, whether they ask for it or not. Ephesians 4:31-32 says, *"Let all bitterness and wrath and anger and clamor and slander be put away from you, along with all malice. Be kind to one another, tender-hearted, forgiving each other, just as God in Christ also has forgiven you."*

A dear lady at church told me, "I did what you said and approached a woman who hurt me. I told her that I forgive her, and do you know what she said? She said, 'Okay.' She just said 'Okay.' Can you believe that? Now I'm madder than ever, because I thought when I forgave her she would apologize for what she had done!" That, however, is the point: you forgive people even when they *don't* ask for it. Most people won't admit or don't even know they've done wrong. Forgiveness isn't for that other person. It's for you.

If you're wondering if God can turn your bitterness around, He absolutely can. Look at what happened in Naomi's life after she let her bitterness go. She eventually trusted God again and helped guide Ruth into a new relationship with a man named Boaz. Boaz was a good man, very wealthy, who actually purchased a plot of land for Naomi. After their marriage, Ruth and Boaz had a child who went on to have a son named Jesse. Jesse grew up to be the father of David, who became the king of Israel. Naomi not only got her land back, but she became part of a great lineage.

A situation may have made you bitter. The devil may be telling you that you have the right to be bitter because of the legitimate wrong you endured. But if you're sitting around nursing your bitterness, then you're looking horizontally and missing the bigger picture. You need to start looking up at God instead of out toward people. If your parents, employer, or anybody else has put a lid on your life, I hope you'll get out of that bondage. Confess your hurt and bitterness to God and allow yourself to get free. Good things *can* come from bad circumstances if we trust God and keep bitterness from eating away at our faith.

Chapter Three

The Ghost of Guilt

You Can't Hide From God

I t sits on top of your shoulders all day long, wherever you go. It's that annoying gnat on hot summer day that flies around your face or gets stuck in your lip gloss. You take it to bed with you and then share your morning cup of coffee with it. If you've ever felt the ghost of guilt, you know exactly what I'm talking about. Guilt was one of the first emotions to come along after the fall of man, when sin entered the world. Man quickly sinned—and guilt quickly followed.

Adam and Eve had everything they could ever need, but it wasn't enough. God had told them they could eat any fruit from any tree in the entire garden, except one. You would think that wouldn't have been a problem. But the fruit on that forbidden tree not only was their downfall, but also the downfall of mankind! Isn't it like us always to want what we can't have? Instead of being able to enjoy all that God had given them, Adam and Eve become focused on the one thing they aren't supposed to have. So Eve, believing the serpent's lie that the fruit will make her as wise as God, eats and gives some to Adam. They experience shame and guilt for the first time.

Later, God asks them, *"Where are you?"* Adam yells out from behind a bush, *"I was afraid because I was naked and so I hid."* God asks him, *"Who told you that you're naked? Have you eaten from the tree I told you not to?"* Like a lot of us do when the heat is turned up, Adam quickly blames someone else. He tells God, *"The woman, you gave me, she did it."* He not only blames Eve for telling him to eat the fruit, but he also blames God for giving Eve to him in the first place. Adam says, *"God, it was all Eve's fault . . . Oh and by the way, God, remember You're the One who gave her to me!"* Talk about a world-class blamer! Next, God asks Eve, *"What is it you've done?"* Taking a cue from Adam, she blames the serpent (Genesis 3).

If you're not familiar with the rest of the story, Adam and Eve are kicked out of the Garden of Eden. This is how sin is born and then passed on to everyone thereafter. Sin entered the world with full force and brought its tag team partner, guilt, along with it. Before Adam and Eve disobeyed God, they had spent time with Him every day. God would stroll leisurely around the garden with them. Adam and Eve relished the time they spent with God, enjoying just getting to hang out and talk with Him every day. The terms "naked" or "shame" were not meaningful to them before sin.

But something changes after they eat the fruit. The closeness and fellowship that they had with God is disrupted, and they experience a new feeling when He visits them. They go from being best friends with God to feeling like they need to hide from Him. The Bible says that after eating the fruit, "...
their eyes were opened ..." (Gen. 3:7). All of their innocence is stripped away. John Calvin once said in his Commentary on Genesis Volume 1, "They felt shame, their conscience was awakened, and their guilt was triggered." It isn't that they feel guilty being naked. They feel guilty because they have disobeyed God. Adam and Eve think that if they can cover up their bodies, then maybe they can cover up the sin and shame they feel. However, they quickly realize that their new pal, Guilt, isn't easy to shake.

Anyone Got Any Loin Cloths I Can Borrow?

My oldest son, BJ, has the purest heart of anyone I know. He truly has a heart of gold. As the firstborn, I'm sure he had it a little harder than my other two boys. Outside of our home, BJ was very quiet as a kid. People used to ask his brothers, "Man, does your brother ever talk? He never says a word!" That came as a big surprise to me, because BJ was always talking and laughing about something at home. He used more words in a day then all of the rest of us combined.

Now that he's grown and out of the house, I recently found out why he was so quiet in school. According to BJ, I told him that he needed to be a good little boy and not talk in class unless the teacher was talking to him. Bless his heart, being the obedient child that he was, he wouldn't even talk to his classmates during free time! That just shows you the kind of kid he was; he listened to his mom and me no matter what! He never rocked the boat and always wanted to do as he was told. That's how we knew something was very wrong one day when he seemed anxious when he came home from school.

When BJ was in kindergarten, all the kids in his class started sporting these Tony the Tiger locks on their belt loops. It was the prize in the bottom of the Frosted Flakes cereal box at the time, and BJ wanted one terribly! He ate and ate and ate the cereal until he could eat no more, but he never found the lock. One day at school, he was walking by the teacher's desk and noticed a gleaming, yellow object. He looked more closely and saw that it was a Tony the Tiger lock! Mesmerized by the toy he had been hunting down for weeks, BJ quickly looked over his shoulder and snatched the thing up!

When he came home from school that day, I noticed the lock attached to his belt loop . . . quite a fashion statement for the little guy! I was so happy for him, thinking he had finally eaten his way to victory! I said, "BJ, you finally got that lock, huh? I know you're thrilled!" My praise was too much for my little soldier's conscience to take, and he busted out crying! Before I could say anything else, he spilled the beans and told us the whole story. The guilt had eaten away at him all day, and you could see it on his red, tear-stained face. The next day my wife, Debbie, walked him into the classroom and watched as he handed the lock over and apologized to

51

his teacher. His conscience was clear, and he could relax and be a little boy again.

Sometimes we don't own up to our guilt quite as fast as BJ did. Sometimes it can take weeks, months, even years to admit our wrong. When we don't admit our guilt, we try to take the load off by hiding. Adam and Eve feel this way when they make loincloths for themselves (Gen. 3:7). They really hope that it will cover up their sins and their guilt, but of course it does not. Just like Adam and Eve, we work to cover our own bad deeds, making our own set of loincloths. Here are four ways that we try to hide from our sin:

1. Rationalize Guilt
2. Deny Responsibility
3. Run Away
4. Increase Responsibility

We attempt to rationalize our guilt. We blame our bad behavior on rude employers or horrible teachers. The excuses just keep on coming. We blame others, not ourselves. Adam and Eve handle guilt like they are playing hot potato. "It's not my fault; it's hers," or "It's not my fault; it's that snake's." Instead of owning our mistakes, we rationalize our responsibility.

We deny responsibility. Do you remember King Saul? He was guilty of disobedience. God told him to kill the Amalekites, their king, and sheep, but Saul did not. When Samuel confronted him about his disobedience, he said, *"What then is this bleating of sheep in my ears?"* (1 Sam. 15:14). Even though Saul disobeyed God, he flat out denies his responsibility. He plays the blame game. Saul blames his disobedience on the poor sheep! [AUTHOR: this section is a bit unclear.]

We run from guilt. Often we try and get as far away from the feeling of guilt as possible. In the Bible, Judas literally runs from his guilt. He throws down the money he had been given for betraying Jesus and then hangs himself. He was trying to run away from the guilt he felt.

We increase religious activity. Some of the most faithful, religious people are actually guilt-driven. When they sin, they "step it up" in church activities. On the outside, they seem like they've got everything together; but inside, they're hoping that their sin won't be found out, like a hamster spinning his wheel. This type of person usually comes out hard against the very sin that haunts them. It's an attempt to keep the spotlight off their own life and shift it to someone else.

The problem is that none of these methods works to resolve guilt; they just increase fear. As soon as God asks Adam where he is, he says, "I was afraid" (Gen. 2:10). This is the ghost of guilt coming into the picture.

False Guilt vs. True Guilt

Sam was a seventeen-year-old high school student with a twelve-year-old little brother, Jamie. Sam loved Jamie and was very protective of his younger sibling. There wasn't anything in the world that Sam wouldn't do for Jamie. One afternoon, the family was headed out of town to visit some relatives in another state, and the two brothers were seated in the back row of the family's SUV.

The family noticed blue and red flashing lights straight ahead. Apparently, a few minutes earlier someone had run their car off the road. As they passed by the wreck and ambulance, Sam asked Jamie to move to the row in front of them so both boys could buckle up and still stretch out and have their own space. In the back of his mind, Sam also thought that the middle row was probably a safer place to sit, and Sam always was looking out for his younger brother. Sam had no way to know what lay ahead.

No more than five minutes after passing the car accident, an oncoming car began to drift into the family's lane. Sam and Jamie's father made a desperate attempt to avoid the car headed straight toward them. The family held on tight and braced themselves for a head-on collision. Tragically, Jamie was killed instantly.

Obviously, Sam was completely devastated at the loss of his little brother, as anyone would be. But what haunted him even more was a feeling of responsibility. Sam had, minutes before the wreck, asked his brother to switch seats; in Sam's mind, it was because Jamie was sitting where he was that he was killed. He accepted all the guilt and just couldn't forgive himself. Day after day, month after month, he wondered what might have happened if only he hadn't told Jamie to move into the other seat.

You and I understand that there was no way Sam could have known his brother was going to be killed. His motives were pure, and he was looking out for his brother. It wasn't his fault that the mid-section of the car didn't handle the force of the accident as well as it should have. Sam had no control over the situation, but he thought he did and blamed himself. Sam was experiencing false guilt.

False guilt is a feeling of responsibility for something that you cannot control. If you have ever experienced false guilt, I'm sure you can empathize with Sam. You know the pressure false guilt puts on you and how it eats at you throughout the day. False guilt lies to you, saying, "You could have done something" or "You should feel bad about this." False guilt tells you that you are responsible, even when logic proves that you've done nothing wrong. False guilt is a burden that you are not meant to carry. God never intended for us to feel false guilt.

False guilt often comes from others' judgments and suggestions. Someone may disapprove of you or your actions and then try to make you feel ashamed. You know the kind of people that put false guilt on you. They say things like, "Well, it must be nice to drive a car like that," or "Oh . . . you got that promotion; you must think you're a superstar now," and "We can't all be as good as you." I just want to say to these kinds of people, "No, you can't, not with an attitude like that." They want to make you feel guilt for your success.

Often, in marriage, one spouse will try to place guilt on the other by going over their faults. I've heard husbands say things like, "She never cleans the house and doesn't have dinner ready on time like my mom used to." Ladies, if your husband says this to you, I suggest you take the approach my daughter-in-law once used on my son. Soon after my son got married, he and his wife came over for a visit. Debbie and I were talking to them about their honeymoon and finding out how their first few weeks as a married couple had been.

My son said, "I love being married, and I've found out that there isn't much I didn't know about Carrie. But she sure doesn't keep the refrigerator stocked like Mom did. And I've run out of clean boxers twice." Without missing a beat, my daughter-in-law said with a smile, "Then I guess you'll be sleeping at your Momma's house tonight, since you like it so much better." Ladies, try that one next time and I bet those ungrateful husbands will get the point. Don't put false guilt on your spouse. Tell your spouse how important they are to you and how much you need them in your life. False guilt will only strain your relationship.

Do not allow others to chip away at your self-worth. Your value, or self-worth, should not come from people; it should come from God. I mean think about it . . . God believes you are valuable enough to have sent His Son to earth to die for you. If that doesn't let you know how special you are, then I don't know what will. God didn't have to sacrifice His Son on your behalf; and if He didn't believe you were worth it, He probably wouldn't have. You are valuable in God's eyes.

Don't believe the lies others are telling you. Start telling yourself each morning, "I am a great wife" or "I am a great husband." Remind yourself daily that you are an awesome parent, a caring boss, or a loyal employee. Whatever your false guilt might be, counter it with the truth. You may feel sometimes like you could have been a better parent. You may worry that you should have spent more time with your children when they were little. We all second-guess ourselves from time to time; but if we allow that to build up, it can quickly turn into false guilt. However, if the facts are that you have a great relationship with your children, your children turned out well, and they even tell you regularly what a good parent you are to them, then believe that. Don't let false guilt stand in the way of the facts.

Sometimes your own parent can make you feel false guilt. You may spend a lot of time with your aging parent, take care of them financially, or even help them out with their daily chores. But I've seen many people who do all these things for their parents, and yet the parents still make their grown children feel guilty for not doing more. Don't fall for it. If the facts don't line up, don't believe the accusations.

As with Sam's story, guilt sometimes follows grief. When people lose a loved one, they often ask, "Did I do enough?" Perhaps they wonder, "If I had only . . ." With false guilt, a person who hasn't actually done anything wrong still feels guilty, even after confessing whatever sin they think they've committed. Confessing false guilt does not lead one to feel peace or God's forgiveness. God definitely never wants His children to experience this false sense of guilt. Revelation 12:10 says the devil is *"... the accuser of the brethren ..."* It means that he accuses without cause. There's no reason you should feel guilty, but he still tries to manipulate you into feeling that you should. He tells you that God won't forgive you and makes you feel guilty for something you haven't done wrong.

I heard a story about a single mom who had two young boys. These boys stayed in trouble, not behaving for one second. Whenever there was any mischief happening in the neighborhood or at school, her boys were always the ones involved. At her wits' end one day, the mother asked her preacher for help. She told him that she was a single mom doing the best she could, but was afraid that her boys' bad behavior was leading them down the wrong path. The pastor agreed to try to help. He told her to bring the younger son by his office first, so he could try to scare him a little bit. Put the fear of God in him, so to speak. So the lady dropped him off at the pastor's office.

The little boy sat nervously across the desk from the preacher, not quite knowing what to expect. Then the preacher told the boy how God watches our every move and knows everything we do. He told the little guy that it's impossible to hide from God, because He is always watching. By now, the boy was feeling a little anxious. The preacher then said, "Son, where is God?" Not knowing how to answer, the boy just sat there in silence. The preacher raised his voice and said loudly, "Where is God?" At this point, the little boy was completely nervous. He didn't know what to say. The preacher then thought, "I'll just scare him a little." So he got up and walked over to the boy. He leaned over him and said in a deep, strong voice, "SON, I SAID, 'WHERE IS GOD?'" Quickly, the boy leaped out of his chair, dashed past the secretary, and ran all the way back home. He rushed into his brother's room and slammed the door. Out of breath from the run home, he looked up at his brother and said, "We're in BIG trouble! God is missing and they think we had something to do with it."

Now that's what you call false guilt. Sometimes you and I can feel just like this little boy did. We let somebody else make us feel guilty for something that we haven't done wrong. God doesn't want you to get bogged down by false guilt, and is never the cause of those feelings. The devil is using false guilt to keep you discouraged and unable to be the person God wants you to be.

****

True guilt is the only kind of guilt that you should ever feel. It's the guilt that results from breaking one of God's laws. Let's be real—you know when you've done something that you shouldn't have. Romans 2:15 says, ". . *the work of the Law [are] written in their hearts."* It's already been built into us. God uses true guilt to stir our conscience whenever we start veering off track. This is God's alarm system. When you do something wrong, you feel true guilt; your alarm is going off and your conscience is trying to help you do the right thing. Martin Luther, the great preacher and founder of the Reformation, once said, "In preaching, I find it impossible to avoid offending guilty people" (Blue Letter Bible Commentaries, Galatians 3). Isn't that so true? As a pastor, I've found that the people who dislike me most often are feeling true guilt, which is the root of their anger.

King David, the giant killer, wrote about the effects of true guilt after he had an affair with Bathsheba. He describes **feeling convicted because he broke his relationship with God**. True guilt will leave you feeling like you've messed things up with God. David also talks about being **unable to rest** (Psalm 22:2). If you've felt true guilt before, it can disturb your sleep and keep you awake at night. It's hard to keep it off your mind. I heard about a man who was having trouble sleeping because he lied on his tax return. After countless nights of no sleep, he sent the IRS a letter. He wrote, "I've been having trouble sleeping at night because I lied on my taxes, so here's five hundred dollars. If I still can't sleep, I'll send you the other five hundred." Well, that's one way to clear the conscience.

We also learn that David felt **completely overwhelmed and spiritually weakened.** Sometimes when you sin, your guilt keeps you away from your church or the Bible. You think you can avoid facing your guilt. The reality is that this is the time you should make sure you are in church and reading your Bible, because the longer you stay out, the harder it is to come back. Avoiding areas of your life that convict you actually make you weaker and more likely to mess up in the future.

David's guilt also made him **feel distanced from his friends** (Psalm 22:6-7; 11). His friends quit being around him. Why? Because sin makes a person hard to live with. When you're dealing with sin on the inside, it comes out as anger, jealousy, or a bad attitude on the outside. Who wants to associate with that? Pretty soon, no one wanted to be around David.

The good news is that you can get a handle on true guilt by confessing your sin to God. Tell Him where you went wrong and that you're sorry. Just as confessing your sin to God brings forgiveness, confessing your guilt brings peace. Confession will wipe your guilt away. There use to be an old Rolaids commercial: "How do you spell relief?" Well, relief for true guilt comes from giving it to God. If you've been haunted by the ghost of guilt, whether true or false, then go ahead and unload that baggage today. You're carrying a load that God never intended for you, so hand it over to Him. Don't let pride get in your way, but let God set you free.

Chapter Four

The Phantom of Fear

Fearless or Fear Lot?

Don't you just love the feeling of uncertainty? Not knowing what could take place from one moment to the next? Don't the "what if's" in life just thrill you? Excite you? If you believe in Murphy's Law, then you know all the worst-case scenarios that may occur in any situation. And if that's not enough, you've got references. You've heard stories. You either know or have heard of someone who has faced a terrible outcome when placed in your exact situation. If that's not enough to convince you that you better watch out, I don't know what is.

I'm sure you can sense my sarcasm. Who really loves uncertainty? None of us do, right? Of course, most of us would like to know how something is going to turn out before we go ahead with it. But hey—this is life, and we don't always get that privilege. I'm not saying there is anything wrong with wondering what the outcome of a particular situation might be . . . not at all. But don't let the possibility of something going wrong keep you from moving forward. That's called fear. Fear is the last thing God wants in your life.

Fear will keep you from reaching your dreams; it will hold you back and stifle your potential. If you really want to live an average life, then start letting fear sit in the driver's seat. If you are looking for a sure path to a paranoid and dull existence, then let fear drive your life. But I know you better than that, and I'm sure you don't want that for yourself. You want much more, because God didn't create you to be average! He didn't create you to remain stagnant for fear of what could go wrong if you take a risk. He wants you to reach your full potential and achieve your destiny.

Second Timothy 1:7 NLT says, *"For God has not given us a spirit of fear and timidity, but of power, love, and self-discipline"* You weren't designed to be fearful . . . you were designed for power, love, and a sound mind (a self-disciplined mind). A sound mind doesn't listen to the negative voice of fear. A sound mind realizes that God is in control.

Check out what it says in 1 John 4:18 NKJV: *". . . fear involves torment."* If you've been living with fear, then you understand this verse fully. Fear will haunt you and make you feel uneasy. You cannot seem to escape the torment. Everywhere you go, fear seems to follow. Fearful people want to stay in their supposed "safe zone" all day. This may be your house, your side of town, your old friends, your same job, or your long-time boyfriend or girlfriend. You get my point. Fear is the devil's biggest weapon to keep you from becoming all that God intended for you. Did you know *fear* actually means "to draw back from, run away, or be paralyzed by terror"? It comes from the Greek word *phobos,* which is the origin of the word *phobia*. Fear of what *could* happen will keep you paralyzed.

An Internet search of phobias reveals thousands of different sites. For example, *eccliasiphobia* is the fear of church. You probably know a few people who have this one. *Euphobia,* the fear of hearing good news, affects negative people and gossipers. They're the kind of people that throw the remote at the TV when the weatherman says, "It's going to be a beautiful day." I have a friend whose father abandoned him and his mother. Whenever anyone asks about his father, he sardonically retorts, "My dad was *nostophobic."* When people looked perplexed, he informs them, "He had a fear of returning home." *Pentheraphobia* is the fear of mothers-in-law. I know a lot of men with that one! *Venustrophobia* is the fear of beautiful women. I can't say I've ever had that before. And *pantophobia* is the fear of everything, so you literally can have a fear of anything and everything.

Believe it or not, not every fear is bad. There are two types of fear that can be useful. The first one is **positive fear,** which is a respectful fear of God, fear of pride, or a fear of injuring a relationship. All of us should have a healthy fear of God, because He is the One who gives us each breath that we breathe. I believe a healthy fear of God can help you leverage yourself against temptation. It is wise to fear God. The Bible says, *"The fear of the LORD is the beginning of wisdom"* (Ps. 111:10).

The fear of becoming prideful is healthy, because pride will attack your character and eventually be your downfall. God won't bless a lot of people past a certain point, because He knows they'll get prideful. You also could be afraid of injuring a relationship, and there is absolutely nothing shameful about that fear. For example, if you're afraid of hurting your spouse, you're less likely to run off with another woman and ruin your marriage. Children who are afraid to disappoint their parents are less likely to misbehave. That's positive fear.

Another healthy fear is **protective fear,** which is fear of reasonable danger, like snakes or electricity. Notice I said *reasonable* danger. For example, not traveling because of fear of car wrecks is letting fear dictate the amount of life you actually live! But you should have a reasonable protective fear.

We live on a lake, and it's pretty much guaranteed that every time you go down to the boathouse, you'll see a snake. It's never an issue of if you are going to see a snake, but when. I know some people have them as pets, and I apologize in advance, but I can't stand them! They just give me goose bumps. UGH! My wife told me one weekend after witnessing one of my snake encounters, "I've never seen you afraid of anything before, but when I saw you in the yard beating a dead snake over and over, you looked like a lunatic!" She'll tell our boys, "Look at your father! That snake was dead an hour ago, but he's still hitting it with a shovel! It looks like an old limp hose! Go down there and tell your Dad that it's dead so he can give it a rest!" Protective fear is a fear of something that could harm you, a reasonable danger.

Paralyzing fear dictates your every move. It causes you to fear change or risk-taking, always imagining the worst in every situation. A person struggling with paralyzing fear may need to examine their faith. Here's the deal. If things remain safe and unchanged—same job, same relationships, same routine—then you don't hear the voice of fear. You think, "Me? Fearful? Nah!"

It's like when you're flying on an airplane and all of the sudden you hear a new noise. Now everyone on the flight, who claimed to have no fear of flying, starts looking around the plane in paranoia, flagging down the flight attendants and looking to the complete stranger next to them for assurance. In life, when you move out of your comfort zone and don't know what's around the corner, you may then start listening to the voice of fear. That's when people who thought they lived a fearless life start to listen. And if fear knows you're listening, you can bet it will keep talking to you.

Who's in Control of Your Life?

Shadrach, Meshach, and Abednego were three guys who served God faithfully. These three Jewish men were as bold as lions; they were not afraid of anyone, even the bully King Nebuchadnezzar. Nebuchadnezzar wanted to create an elite empire, so he had gone to other countries and brought their wealthiest and smartest people back to Babylon. Unfortunately, he did not take into account that all the foreigners in his country would worship different gods. So ol' Neb devises a plan to get his people in alignment. He builds a golden tower for everyone to worship and threatens that anyone who refuses will be put to death. You see, Neb had a pretty extreme personality.

He wants to let people know that *he* is king and *he* rules their life. He wants them to believe that he controls their destiny and that their future is in his hands, and his hands only. And this is what fear says to you: "I rule your life; I hold your destiny and control your future. You can talk about God all you want; but at the end of the day, you're going to cheat on your taxes because you fear losing money more than you fear God." Fear tells you, "You're going to lie about your product to make that sale, because you fear the economy more than God." Or, "You will compromise your values in that relationship because you fear not being accepted by people more than God."

That's why in Daniel 3:7 it says, ". . . *all the peoples, nations and men of every language fell down and worshiped the golden image Nebuchadnezzar the king had set up.*" Nebuchadnezzar is saying, "I don't care whom you say you worship; because when I show you that it's life or death, you'll change your mind." And guess what? He is right.

Some of the people in Neb's kingdom probably had been claiming that they had stayed true to God; but when it comes time to stand up, they are cowards. They take the easy way out because they are afraid. But Shadrach, Meshach, and Abednego stand firm. They know that their God is the one true God and that He will protect them.

Nebuchadnezzar's scare tactics aren't going to force these guys into worshiping a false God. Their faith is real. These boys believe what the Bible says in Exodus 20:3 KJV: "Thou shalt have no other gods before me." Did you know that centering your life around fear is like worshipping a false god? Paralyzing fear tells God, "I don't trust You, I don't think You have my best interests in mind, and I don't think You can take care of me."

Fear always comes along and asks the question, "What then?" If you're a teenager and don't go along with the crowd, what then? If you take a risk and it doesn't work out, what then? Fear always asks you what will happen if you put your neck on the line. What happens if you lose your job? What happens if he walks out of your life? What happens if you say no? What then? Fear tells you to do the secure thing because it's predictable. If you do what is predictable and safe, you will live to see another day.

But if you go with faith instead of fear . . . what then? What's around the corner? The fact is you don't know what's around that corner either way. I could give you story after story of women who told me, "I knew I shouldn't have married that guy, but I was afraid if I ever spoke up that he would leave me. Down the road, we had two kids. I was working to make ends meet when he left me. Now I'm still alone, but have two kids to raise. I succumbed to my fear, but fear didn't give me what it promised."

Sometimes when we listen to fear, we create the very problem we were trying to prevent. Sometimes we live our life trying to "play it safe." Yet the reality is you don't really have any guarantee that *anything* is safe. You may lose your job anyway. You may lose your spouse anyway. Fear makes you try to achieve security, when you really can't. If God is leading you to a new job, don't let fear keep you from it. You might think, "Yeah, but I have friends and family here and this is secure." Nothing is a sure thing; you don't know what the future holds. If you're dating someone you're not that into because you are afraid of being alone, then don't let that fear keep you from meeting the right person. If you stay in the wrong relationship, you could end up alone anyway.

Nebuchadnezzar convinces everyone but Shadrach, Meshach, and Abednego that he is in control of their lives. Fear does the same thing. It lies to you and tries to convince you that if you don't give into it, things are not going to turn out in your favor. King Nebuchadnezzar tries to use fear to control Shadrach, Meshach, and Abednego. They are brought before the king for questioning about their refusal to bow before his image, which they admit. The king tries to give them a second chance before throwing them into the furnace. A lot of people might have reconsidered at this point, but they basically say, "Look, Neb, the problem isn't that we didn't understand you the first time. We heard you loud and clear, but we're just not gonna do it. We know the true God" (Daniel 3). They didn't let fear control their life. You shouldn't either.

God Is Able

Are you going to trust the one who thinks he is in control or the One who actually *is* in control? We always fear what's around the corner. Why? What if something better than we could have ever hoped for is around that corner? Like success, better health, or greater opportunities. But you'll never know if you listen to the voice of fear.

Shadrach, Meshach, and Abednego choose to let faith navigate their lives rather than fear. They went toe-to-toe with the king and told him, *". . . our God whom we serve is able to deliver us from the burning fiery furnace, and He will deliver us from your hand, O king"* (Dan. 3:17 NKJV). These guys were willing to die for their faith rather than succumb to fear. They knew God would protect them. They were saying, "King, we don't know the outcome, but we are going to trust the One we know controls the future, not the one who thinks he does."

Recently, I was talking to a friend in south Florida, who just got into selling real estate. He told me, "Bill, everybody was telling me not to get into real estate right now and how bad the market was. They kept telling me that I would starve if I got into it . . . but I'm selling houses like a mad man down here! I can't keep one on the market!" He didn't put his trust in what everybody around him thought; he put his trust in God. He knew that the final authority on whether he sold any houses or not was not the market or other people. It was God. If there is some fear in your life that's keeping you crippled, then I want you to catch this. There is more security in God, the One who is able, than anything or anyone else who thinks they can control your life.

There are a lot of good people who are so afraid of what's around the corner that they barricade themselves within their own lives. Anchored down by their fear, they are unable to move forward. In their minds, the unknown always equals tragedy. They believe the only way to keep safe is to avoid the unknown. However, giving into fear and avoiding a leap of faith are not guarantees that things are going to work out. If you surrender to fear, you still might lose that job. You still might lose that relationship. There is no guarantee. You need to realize that God is in control. He's the One who controls your future.

Every great victory is the result of courage in the face of fear. Winston Churchill stood up against Nazi Germany. Rosa Parks took a stand by taking a seat in the front of the bus. We wouldn't have a Protestant church today if it weren't for the great reformer, Martin Luther. He preached that people should be able to have their own personal relationship with Christ and their own Bible in their hands. Martin Luther King, Jr., stood up and fought segregation. The night before he was assassinated, he said "I'm not worried about any man, I'm not fearing anything." When these fearless men and women stood up, others received victories as well. Every time you reject your fear, you make a breakthrough for someone else.

You need to decide to stand up, turn the tide, and not let fear conquer your life. You stand to lose everything if you go along with the crowd and your fear. Shadrach, Meshach, and Abednego understand this. They put their faith in God, not fear. When ol' Neb throws the boys into the furnace, he thinks he is controlling their future. Fear does the same thing to you. Neb had thought they would figure out that their fate was in his hands, but boy is he wrong!

Neb notices another person in the fire with Shadrach, Meschach, and Abednego. Puzzled, he says to his servant, "Didn't we only throw three into the furnace?" (Dan. 3:24). When the servant confirms that it had been three men, the king says, "I see four men, unbound, walking around in the fire unharmed! And the fourth looks like a god" (Dan. 3:25). God Himself is with Shadrach, Meshach, and Abednego in the fiery furnace that day; and just like He was with those three guys, He'll be with you when you're going through the fire. All you have to do is ignore the voice of fear and put your faith in God.

Shadrach, Meshach, and Abednego survive the fire and come out completely unscathed. There are no ashes on their clothes, no hair on their head out of place, not even the smell of smoke on their clothes. This leads King Nebuchadnezzar to change the law, tear down the idol and declare that their God is the one true God. Ironic isn't it? Just like Neb, when fear knows it has lost, then it will give up and you will be able to live a free life.

Shadrach, Meshach, and Abednego hadn't known what God was going to do, but they did know He was able. Do you believe that your God is big enough to take care of your problems? Do you believe that no matter what comes into your life, your God is able? I had a sweet lady say to me, "Pastor, I hear what you're saying, but you don't understand. My son is in a lot of trouble." My answer was, "Well, is God able?" If God is able, then we need to start listening to the One who is in control instead of the ones that try to convince us they're in control. Decide today that whenever the voice of fear tries to break into your thoughts, you'll say, "I am not going to fear anymore. Why am I afraid? God knows what's around the corner and is big enough to take care of me." You need to tell fear to go find somebody else to torment. When you really believe that God is in control of your destiny, you will experience a new kind of freedom. You'll be able to walk through storms in your life and come out unharmed on the other side. You'll be able to sleep in peace.

A couple of years ago, some people over the age of ninety completed a survey on what they would do differently if they could live their life over. Of all the possibilities, these three main answers were given (Dr. Anthony Campolo, Eastern College, Pennsylvania).

#1—Reflect more. Don't run through life like it is a sprint. Watch more sunsets, enjoy better food, and laugh more. When you start looking at your photo albums and scrapbooks, you will think, "Where did the time go?" Take a moment each day to enjoy your life, your spouse, your children, or your grandchildren. Make memories in the small, seemingly insignificant moments.

#2—Take more risks. Take more chances and live life out on the edge. Travel, do things you've always wanted to do, even things that scare you. There's no point in always playing it safe. The truth is that unless Jesus comes back first, none of us are making it out alive. If you're afraid of something, go do it! My wife was a little fearful of adventure when we first got married, so I decided to change that. I took her parasailing one Thanksgiving. Years later, I took her skiing, not on the bunny slopes — we conquered the black slopes! My wife will tell you today that she's shocked she's still alive and kicking after all the crazy things we've done together. But she is, isn't she? That's the whole point. She's doesn't live by fear anymore. When you go to heaven, God will not say, "What are you doing here? You're not supposed to be here today." Too many people have spent their life holding on instead of letting go.

#3 — Do something that really matters. Do something that lives on long after you die. Don't dabble, do something that really matters. Make a positive mark on the world. Leave your footprints in the sands of time.

I really believe that this is good advice. The bottom line is who's in control? Who do you trust? Lately when I've been driving around town, I've noticed a bunch of new billboards that simply read, "Trust God." My question to you is this: Are you going to trust the economy or God? Are you going to trust relationships or God? Are you going to trust those that think they're in control or the One who really is? Don't spend your life in fear. Trust the One who is able to decide your future. If you can say, "God is still able," then you will destroy fear and be able to enjoy your life. This is the day that you need to say good-bye to fear and realize that in your life, God is able.

Chapter Five

The Acid of Anger

I'm So Mad!

Acid can eat away flesh, layer by layer, until it reaches bone. Anger is no different. Acid can dissolve the very container that holds it, and anger will do the very same thing if it enters your life. It will creep its way into your soul and begin devouring everything in you that's good. Anger eats away at your reasoning and will cause you to make foolish mistakes. Have you ever tried to talk to an angry person? You can't!

Anger makes people unreasonable. It will eat away at your mind, your heart, and your body. Doctors will tell you that anger can cause high blood pressure, heart disease, headaches, nerve conditions, lack of sleep, and a host of other health problems. Every time you turn on the news, there are tons of anger-fueled stories of theft, rape, murder, and war. Anger causes all sorts of chaos. Where violent crimes and chaos exist, there is anger. Did you know the first murder in the Bible was actually caused by anger? Man hadn't been on this planet half a minute before anger came on the scene.

Adam and Eve had two sons, the apples of their eyes. As the only two kids on the planet, I bet Cain and Abel played together all the time. I have three sons, and I can remember sitting back when my boys were little and just watching them play together. They would explore the unknown, pretend to be super heroes, wrestle, and sometimes work together as a team. Nothing was more entertaining or could make my heart melt like watching my sons love one another. I bet Adam and Eve felt exactly the same—until something changed along the way. As the days, months, and years pass, Cain becomes more and more resentful, believing he is always playing second fiddle to Abel. Cain is sure Abel is his parents' favorite and feels like nothing he does is ever good enough. Why can't he be more like Abel? These thoughts plague Cain's mind night and day, until the resentment boils and festers into full-blown anger. This anger puts Cain on the edge. It won't take much send him over now.

One day, the two brothers present their individual offerings to God. Cain brings an offering of the fruit from the ground, while Abel brings the firstborn of his sheep. God respects Abel's offering, but not Cain's. Cain is furious! Isn't it just like Abel to always get all of the attention? In Cain's eyes, even *God* seems to favor his brother over him. This is the straw that breaks the camel's back. Cain cannot control his feelings any longer; he's had it with being second-best!

The next thing you know, Cain attacks his brother and kills him while they are together in the field (Gen. 4:3-8).

Surely, Cain had loved his brother at one time. They had enjoyed playing together when they were little boys. There were times when they had laughed together and worked together. But like an untreated cancer, Cain's anger toward his brother grow deeper and deeper. Cain's growing resentment and competitive spirit ultimately lead him to commit the unimaginable.

Anger knocks Cain's life right off course. No more birthday parties together. No more adventures together. No more climbing trees or playing hide and seek. No more long walks or meaningful conversations together. No more relationship. No more best friend. All of the good times they could have had in the future are no longer possible. Cain is left with only the memory of faded expectations of things that could have been. Anger destroys Cain's future with Abel, and if we're not careful, anger can destroy our future as well. Anger does not have to end in murder to cause a lot of damage.

Anger is a hostile emotional response. Think about the last time you got angry. Usually mild irritation changes quickly into indignation. You feel the need to act. You think,

"I have to do something about this!" Resentment can easily turn into anger. Maybe you feel like you don't get any credit at work, no matter how hard you try. Things might seem like they always work out for your coworker, but not you. Resentment begins to build up, and much like Cain, you develop a blinded desire to harm that other person in some way.

Anger comes from unresolved hurts, whether real or imagined. Ever been left out? Maybe you weren't invited to a social gathering by a person you considered a close friend. Or what about that time you thought you heard your coworkers gossiping about you? These unresolved hurts can fuel anger.

Anger can come from your worldview. There are some cultures outside of America that actually reward anger. The angrier you are, the better. Some people think life is supposed to be fair; when it isn't, they get angry. Others imagine people are out to get them, so they try to get *them* first. What a paranoid and unhealthy way to live!

Anger also can come from learned patterns. Proverbs 22:24-25 NKJV says, *"Make no friendship with an angry man, . . . lest you learn his ways and set a snare for your soul."* When I first got into ministry, I had an opportunity to work for a great church in Florida. I was praying about it and asking God for guidance and wisdom for weeks beforehand. The morning before I went to the interview, I came across this passage in Proverbs while I was doing my devotion. For some reason or another, it stuck out to me and stayed on my mind all morning.

I went to the interview and things went well . . . until the interview was over. When the pastor was walking me out of his office, his secretary stopped him. She whispered to him about something that had occurred among the staff, and he became enraged! Immediately, without even stopping to consider the fact that I was standing there, he took his hands and raked everything off her desk onto the floor. Almost instantly, I heard that verse in my head: "Make no friendship with an angry man, . . . lest you learn his ways . . ." (Prov. 22:24-25). I knew God was telling me no. The interview had gone really well and I was offered the position, but I wasn't supposed to be there. If I had accepted it, then I probably would have ended up just like him. I'm so glad I listened to what God was telling me and didn't associate with an angry person.

Remember to be careful as you choose your acquaintances. Just like the flu or a virus, we pick up the spirit of those we're around. If you hang out with negative people, you're likely to become negative as well. If you hang out with people who love to eat all the time, there's a good chance you will gain a little weight. If you hang out with adventurous people, you'll probably find yourself taking more risks. You are likely to become similar to those around you, so be careful not to associate with people who are quick to anger. This should include your dating life. Don't date an angry person . . . what good can come of that? If he's angry when you're just dating, imagine how much worse it will get when you are married and live together 24/7. Remember the words of Maya Angelou, when someone shows you who they are, believe them the first time.

An angry person creates a bad environment. You don't want to be involved with hot-tempered people. You'll never be able to relax. You'll spend your days constantly walking on eggshells . . . and what in the world is fun about that? I know you want better for your life, so be careful about the people you choose for it.

The Express Lane

How do you express anger? Is it easy to tell when the angry bug has bitten you, or does it take someone with a doctorate in psychology to figure it out? I bet you can think of at least one or two people who, when they get angry, start whining, as if pouting will resolve all of their issues. You know the ones. They revert into crybaby mode; and every time they get angry, you have to change their diaper. When they go to a restaurant, their reservation can be found under name "Pity" . . . party of one.

Other people withdraw when they're angry. They don't tell you they are angry; they make you try to figure it out on your own. They withdraw from the group and keep to themselves. They wait for others to come pat them on the back and say, "Poor baby . . . bless your heart." Even if they are forty years old, they still expect you to baby them. They're using **isolation** to express their anger.

Another way we express our anger is through **domination.** Have you ever come across somebody who exploits his authority every time he gets a chance? He wants you to know he is the boss. Some people can't afford even a little bit of power, because it goes straight to their head. I used to love watching *The Andy Griffith Show*. I mean, any show that can start off with two minutes of nothing but whistling is something special. Barney, the clumsy, power-hungry deputy, was a real trip! Andy would only give Barney one bullet for his gun because Barney whipped it out every chance he got. Andy was afraid he might shoot someone! Barney loved to throw his weight around. How many Barneys do you know in your own life? Barneys are the ones that get the promotion to become supervisor and then make life miserable for everybody. They run around with their badge, hollering, "I'm the boss! I'm the boss!"

A few years ago I was staying with some friends, and the husband began asking me some questions about the Bible. He told me that he had read recently that the man is supposed to be the head of the household and wives are to submit to their husbands. I will never forget what happened next. It was really late when we were talking, and the rest of the house was asleep. I told him that he was correct, and my buddy ran to the bottom of the staircase and yelled, "Honey, I'm the man of the house! Get out of bed and come down here and get me some water!" Now first off, anybody who's got to tell you he's the man of the house probably isn't, right?

Then I just about fell on the floor laughing when I heard his wife holler back, "Shut up and get your own water!" She told me later that she was not going to spring into action just because he thought he found a badge he could wear. My friend went to church; but instead of finding God, he found a verse he could go home and use to club his wife. He was trying to dominate, but ended up appearing weak.

The third way we express anger is by **retaliating.** This is what Cain did to Abel. Cain killed Abel because of the anger that was in his heart. Anger kept digging at him, nipping at him, and eating away at him until he couldn't take it any longer. He let it go way too far! Proverbs 16:32 NKJV says, *"He who is slow to anger is better than the mighty, and he who rules his spirit than he who takes a city."* Don't react to everything. An old football rule says that the second man always gets penalized. If you get pulled off sides, then you get penalized rather than the player who provoked you. You have to be cautious and learn to handle your anger.

Proverbs 29:22 NKJV says, *"An angry man stirs up strife, and a furious man abounds in transgression."* Proverbs 17:19 says, *"He who loves transgression loves strife."* Whenever you see a person with unmanaged anger, you'll always see chaos and turmoil. They're always creating strife.

Everything is going great; but before you know it, they come in and set the environment to their temperament.

A person with uncontrolled anger always blames others. That's why Cain replied, "Am I my brother's keeper?" when God came to him after the murder and asked, "Where is your brother?" (Gen. 4:9). Literally, anger always blames somebody else. It was their fault . . . they made me angry . . . they hurt me . . . they were wrong!

Anger chains you to your offenders. If you're angry with someone, you'll carry him with you wherever you go. An old culture had a tradition of chaining murderers to their victims and dropping them into the ocean. They would die, strapped face-to-face with the person they murdered. Did you know that if you're angry with someone, but you can't let it go or get past it, you're chained to him? You can be on vacation, traveling around the world, yet still thinking about how angry you are at *him*. Does he deserve to go on vacation with you? Of course not! Even though there's a beautiful sunset and the waves are crashing along the shore, you can't get him off your mind. You wasted all of your best time dwelling on him. That's unresolved anger, my friend. It chains you to the source of your anger, and forces you to keep reliving the hurt, instead of dispelling and releasing it.

People often wonder what the Bible says about anger. Ephesians 4:26 says, *"Be angry, and yet do not sin . . ."* It's alright to get angry; the Bible actually gives you permission, but you must keep it under control. If you get mad, then say you're mad. If you get offended, then say you're offended. Conversations should be direct. You should be able to approach someone who's angered you, and tell him you're mad and tell him why. That's good communication.

But communication can be hard . . . especially when it's between a man and a woman. I hear women say all the time that the men in their life just don't understand them. You know what I say to that? No, they don't. Husbands do not understand their wives. No one understands a woman. It's not a put down; you're God's greatest creation. After God created man, He said, "I can do better than that," and He created woman. But men and women are totally different. You've got to tell men everything. I've heard women sometimes complain that their man missed their anniversary. Well, did you tell him? Did you remind him or did you keep it a secret in hopes that he would remember all on his own? What did you expect? You think he should just know? He doesn't know! He's a man!

Men are real easy. You just feed them and tell them. That's it! Feed them and tell them. There's a story about a guy who was offered one wish by God. God said to him, "I'll give you one wish. What do you want?" The man said, "I really want to go to Hawaii, but I'm afraid to fly and I don't like boats. So would You build me a highway to Hawaii?" God said, "I don't know, that's a lot of work. Is there anything else you want?" The man replied, "Well, I've already been through four wives. Everyone says I don't understand women, so could you help me understand them?" God looked back at him and said, ". . . About that highway—do you want two lanes or four?"

The secret is that you have to tell a man exactly how he has hurt your feelings; and men, you have to do the same thing with your wives. You'll have a healthier relationship when you can communicate clearly with one another.

****

The good news about anger is that you're not the only one who's ever gotten angry. Jesus even got angry. In fact, Mathew 23 is an entire chapter on Jesus' anger. When Jesus was angry, He said, "You are of your father the devil . . ." (John 8:44). Now, this is holy Jesus we're talking about.

Holy, perfect, sinless Jesus got angry. That tells me that it's okay to get angry, as long as we don't let it turn into sin.

If you're angry with someone, don't let it go unresolved. If you're angry with your spouse, don't let the sun go down without resolving the issue. It might mean that you have to stay awake for three days, but don't go to sleep without fixing it. I met a lady a couple years ago whose son was twenty-four years old; she told me that she and her husband hadn't slept in the same bed since her son was born. You don't have to be a rocket scientist to see that something's not right there. Somewhere there was unresolved anger and poor communication. For them, it was easier to sleep in separate rooms for the rest of their lives than to try to resolve the issue. God didn't design marriage to be like that. Don't give the devil the opportunity to exploit you.

Having self-control is the key to keeping your anger in check. One of the most beautiful things to watch in action is self-control. How long is the delay between information coming into your brain and words coming out of your mouth? Do you think about things before you speak? I know that's age-old advice, but it could not be more effective. Use self-control to delay your words from coming out of your mouth until you've thought them through.

My wife is very wise in this area. She practices extreme self-control when choosing what to say and what not to say. Debbie has a rule I love: what she's saying has to be kind, true, and necessary, or she will not speak it. Think about that next time you're tempted to really let someone have it. Is what you're about to say kind, true, *and* necessary? If it's not all three, then don't say it. It may be true, but is it necessary? It may be necessary, but is it kind? This is the kind of self-control that will keep your anger in check. It will help you speak with less haste and more wisdom.

Arming Yourself Against Anger

I hope I haven't given you the impression that anger is always a bad thing. It's not! Trust me, there will come a time when your anger is justified. Sometimes you *should* be upset! You should express your anger. When God's church is wronged, anger is justified. If you have been a victim of physical, sexual, or emotional abuse, then obviously your anger is justified. If you're walking down the street and see a man violating a woman, you are right to get angry and step in. If you witness a child being harmed, you are right to be angry. Sometimes the church becomes a victim and is attacked or wronged in some way. There's nothing wrong with you getting angry and taking up for your church.

Moses was the meekest man in the world, but he wasn't weak. There's a huge difference between being meek and being weak. Weakness means being a sissy . . . but meekness means strength under control. Meekness is being able to contain your strength; it's power with self-control. A good example of meekness is the old Budweiser commercial, in which these six, massive Clydesdales pulled a tiny little wagon. Now, the wagon was so small that a Shetland pony could have pulled it just as easily. In reality, one of those Clydesdales alone could have yanked the entire wagon off and trotted away into the fields if it wanted to, but these horses were showing meekness.

Moses is trying to lead three million griping and complaining Jews into the Promised Land. They can't stop whining for one second. If I were in charge, then I would have saddled up a donkey and left them as soon as they were asleep. "Forget it . . . I've had it up to here . . . Looks like it's just You and me, God. . . . Let 'em spend the next forty years wandering around in the desert alone." But Moses didn't do that because he was meek. When Moses came down from talking with God on top of the mountain, he saw his people building a golden calf to worship. Do you think Moses just stood there? No, he got so angry that he took the Ten Commandments and broke them. God didn't judge him for that. He had a right to be angry. His people had gone haywire. It was time for righteous anger.

A pastor in Atlanta told me about a lady in his church who had gotten arrested. She was eighty years old and charged with assault. Can you imagine? An eighty-year-old woman arrested for assault? She was the sweetest, most godly lady in the church, but one day she got angry. She was in a restaurant eating breakfast, when she overheard two men talking badly about her church. She kept quiet for a moment, making sure her ears were not deceiving her. When she was 100 percent sure of what she was hearing, the little old lady got up and started hitting both men on the head with her pocket book. Maybe a tad extreme, but you get the picture. She experienced righteous anger and decided to take a stand. It's alright to get angry; just remember the Bible says to *sin not.* Don't use your pocket book to beat your offender on the head!

So it's okay to be angry . . . as long as it doesn't cause you sin. Another important factor is how long you hold on to your anger. Do you let it grow and turn into bitterness, or do you know when it's time to let it go? You can keep your anger in check by making sure *NOT* to do these three things:

1. **Don't Repress It:** If you're angry with someone, don't hold it in and pout. Go directly to that person and deal with it.
2. **Don't Suppress It:** When you suppress your anger, you pretend it doesn't exist. It comes out in snide, sarcastic remarks. If the person that offended you asks

about your anger, then don't lie or pretend. Be honest and deal with your feelings.

3. **Don't Express It to Others:** Don't tell everyone at work about your anger. If you're right, you don't have to go rally support. Keep it between you and the offender.

The truth is that the angrier a person is, the more insecure they are. The more insecure a person is, the more irritable they become. Have you ever noticed that a crying baby often quiets as soon as someone picks it up? There are a lot of adults who are crying out to the world in the form of anger. They just want someone to pick them up. They want someone to validate their worth.

Do you know someone who is easily offended? You can offend them by accidentally not noticing that you passed them at church, by not smiling big enough at them, or even by speaking to someone else before you speak to them. Folks, let me help you here—this is caused 100 percent by insecurity. If you're secure in who you are in Christ, then people can't offend you. It just doesn't matter. But if you need other people to validate you in order for you to feel secure, the danger is that other people can take away your validation as well. Look for your security in God and let Him validate you.

You can get freedom over uncontrolled anger by attacking the root of the problem. Figure out exactly what hurt you—not what made you angry, but *why* it hurts the way it does. Anger is a symptom, but hurt is the problem. When you really understand what it is that hurt you, thank God for that hurt in your life. I know it doesn't sound easy, but doing this will make you a better person. If your dad wasn't there for you as a kid, thank God for that experience. Decide that because your dad did not spend time with you as a child, you will be a better dad as a result. Train yourself to thank God not just for the good times, but for the bad times as well. All of your life experiences—the good, the bad, and the ugly—helped shape you into the extraordinary person you are today. The next time anger starts to rise in you, reflect before you react. Ask God to help you avoid those foolish arguments and remember that your pain matters to God. He wants to help—all you have to do is ask.

Chapter Six

The Waste of Worry

Why Worry?

When my three boys were younger, I'd often drive up after work and see them riding their bikes or playing football in the front yard. I saw them do all sorts of fun kid things, but I never saw one of them wringing their hands in worry. I never heard them telling their friends, "Man, I'm so worried about the economy right now. I know I'm only in the third grade, but it's tough out here." They never walked around fretting, "I just don't know if these jeans are gonna last," or "Boy, Dad, what are we gonna do about these gas prices?" My boys never said any of that. Of course they didn't! That would be ridiculous! They never worried about any of those things, because they believed that their dad was going to take care of them. And I did.

You've got to understand that God wants you to feel the same way. He doesn't want you to worry about the economy, your retirement, or anything else for that matter. The last thing God wants you to do is waste your life worrying. He has your best interests in mind. Yeah, He'll make you stretch your faith sometimes. He might even let you get right out to the edge, but He will pull you back in time because He's still watching out for you.

Did you know the word *worry* means "to choke or restrict"? When you start worrying, you feel closed in, as if you don't have any options. It's like going through a maze; at every corner, you're wondering what's next. You feel helpless and hopeless. Have you ever choked on something? Maybe a piece of candy or a popcorn kernel? What did it feel like? Did you begin to panic? Your lungs are still there, still trying to help you breathe, but they can't do their job because something is in the way. It's starting to make sense, isn't it? Just as choking on piece of gum would block your airway and hinder your breathing, worrying and fretting over something hinders your faith. Worrying literally chokes out your faith.

A lot of times we think that we're doing pretty well in the "Sin Department." We say to ourselves, "Man, I'm doing pretty good . . . I've been faithful in my marriage . . . I haven't stole anything . . . I'm a decent parent." But did you know that worrying is a sin? That's right! Last week when you were stressing over your problems at work, you were committing a sin. All the outward good you thought you were doing was negated by your inward worry.

God doesn't want you to worry. God already knows what is going to happen in your life. He's not surprised by anything that comes your way. Nothing comes into your life without permission from God first. He looks at your life from the very end. He's not looking at it from the beginning, wondering what's happening next. He knows the end of the story; He *knows* how you're going to come through it. Quit worrying about what's around the corner and trust the One who knows what the end looks like.

Recall a worry you've had in the past. Remember how anxious you felt? How did it turn out? You're not worrying about it anymore, so God must have taken care of it. You never predicted such a good deal, but that's what you got! God had it all mapped out already, but at the time all you could do was worry about the outcome. The key is to understand that God is standing at the end of your problem and knows exactly how you are going to get through it. Worrying doesn't change anything. No one ever changed the circumstances in their life by worrying—that's why it is such a waste. What can you change by worrying? The fact is you can't control everything in your life. There are uncertainties you can't prevent. So what good does it do to worry?

Worry is a lot like a rocking chair. It'll keep you busy, but won't get you anywhere. George Bernard Shaw said, "The secret to being miserable is to have too much leisure time with nothing to do but worry." There are a lot of good people who intended to enjoy life when they retired, but instead let worry eat their time away. Worry is work. It will tire you out. Some people go to bed exhausted at night because they've been worrying all day long. Believe me, I know them. Worry will become a full-time job if you let it.

Jesus said in Mathew 6:27, *"And who of you by being worried can add a single hour to his life?"* He was letting us know that it's pointless to worry. It doesn't solve anything. How many times have you thought, "Thank goodness I worried about that situation! Boy, I just don't know how I would have got through it, if I hadn't stayed up worrying all night"? Never, because worry only stresses us about things we can't control. God wants you to let go of your worries and relax and know that He really is in control.

Worry's Wrath

Worry has its own plans for your life, which do not include happiness or enjoyment. Worry wants you stressed out, spending your every waking moment on pins and needles. Forget about letting God handle it—what if He doesn't step in and help? What then? This is just the kind of lie that worry will use to deceive you. And if you start listening to worry, it'll wreck your life in more ways than one.

Worry steals your peace like nothing else. It could be a beautiful sunny day without a cloud in the sky. You could have a great family at home. All of your needs could be met; but if you let worry into your heart, then you won't be able to enjoy any of it. You won't be able to enjoy your kids, your spouse, anything. Your peace will be consumed with what's around the corner. You will be bogged down with "What if . . ." questions, and peace will slip out of your hands as you begin to welcome worry into your life.

Doctors tell us that stress affects our sleep, torments our mind, and ruins our health. Have you ever noticed how many different medications there are for stress? It's unbelievable! How many people do you know right now who have to take pills just to make it through the day or night, simply because of worry? Just the other day I spoke to a woman who told me that her doctor had prescribed some very heavy medication to help her deal with stress. She said it all stemmed from her difficult living situation with her husband. What's crazy is that not only is she on drugs, but her kids are on drugs, too!

I thought about that for a moment and then told her, "You guys have this thing all wrong. If he's the problem, give him the drugs! You've got the whole family drugged up." As soon as he wakes up, the whole family, all the way down to little junior starts popping the pills. Something's wrong with this picture. We have entire families heavily medicated over worry and stress. There is no peace anymore. Home is not a place of peace, but a place of pain. That's a problem. We drug ourselves, looking for a way to find peace in our hearts.

Worry will steal peace from your heart in a flash. That's why it says in Matthew 6:25, "*. . . do not be worried about your life . . .*" Don't worry about it. God knows the end of the matter. You're not going to get to heaven one minute before you're supposed to. You're not going to get there and hear, "What happened? How did that get by? Which angel was in charge?" God doesn't have angels running up and down with reports and files on where you are. He knows exactly where you are and what you're going through. And He's not worried. So if He's not worried, why should you be?

Every human being has a certain amount of energy to expend. It's just like our cars. My car will only hold a certain amount of gas, and your car will only hold a certain amount of gas. I can fill my car up and decide that I want to take it to Florida. I can fill it up and just drive it around the block over and over again. Or I can fill it up just to let it idle in the driveway. The thing is, no matter what I do with the gas in my car, it still will burn the gas. It doesn't matter whether I was productive with it or not.

You have a tank of energy within you. You can use it either to be productive or to worry about ten thousand little things. Anger and worry will eat up all of your energy and leave you with no fuel for anything useful. You have to learn to conserve your energy. Athletes understand this concept. They don't practice right before the game starts because they know they have to save their energy for when it counts. Most of the time we fail to do this. We get up and immediately start spending our energy on thinking about a bad news report or something rude a coworker said. By the time we get home to our spouse or kids, we're drained. There's nothing left to give. That's no way to live!

When you get to the end of your life and begin to look back over how you spent the time God gave you, you'll see how much you missed that life had to offer. Instead of enjoying your family, friends, and blessings, you will discover that you wasted all of your energy fretting over the trivial. If that's you, then don't waste your energy on worry for one more second. It may have stolen precious moments of time already; do not let it steal a second more! Make a promise to yourself to start conserving your energy for productivity and things that matter.

Worry will make you take your eyes off of God and forget Him. Jesus said, *"Look at the birds of the air, for they neither sow nor reap nor gather into barns; yet your heavenly Father feeds them. Are you not of more value than they?"* (Matt. 6:26 NKJV). Jesus knew what a stronghold worry would be for us. He knew that even when we are successful in other areas of our lives and seem to have it all together, the enemy would use worry to keep us down. The devil knows your weakness. He may not be able to get you to fall into other traps like lust, greed, or pride. But worry is easy for us to fall into, because we don't realize it is a sin. Jesus was encouraging us in this passage to remember that the birds in the air don't worry about what they will eat next. They simply do what they have always known to do, and God provides for them. The great news for us is that even while the birds are taken care of, Jesus didn't die on the cross for them—He died on the cross for you. Don't you think He's going to take care of you? Sure, He will.

Worry takes your eyes off of God. I love the story of Noah and the ark. Did you know that the one window God had Noah put in the boat was at the top? I think that window is a wonderful word picture for how God wants each of us to live our lives. God didn't want Noah constantly seeing all of the flooding rain, wind, and destruction. He didn't want him focusing on the storm, but looking up and keeping his eyes on Him.

Isaiah 26:3 says, *"The steadfast of mind You will keep in perfect peace, because he trusts in You."* When you go through storms in your life, look at God. Don't focus on the circumstances around you; they will only bring fear into your life. Don't look at the size of your problem; look at the size of your God. He's big enough to take care of it.

Worry wastes your time and energy. Suppose you only have seventy years to live. Let's say that no matter what, if you worry or not, you're going to live until you're seventy years old. Worrying will not give you a second more;

instead, it will steal your peace and take away important moments that you will never be able to get back. Worrying about things will not change the outcome. Enjoy the moment you have right now.

Worrying about the future only wastes your time in the present. God is going to see to it that if you need a raise, you'll get it. If you need a job or relationship, He's going to make sure you get it. Too often we spend way too much time trying to help God drive. God is in control when He is at the wheel of your life. The bumper stickers that say, "God is my co-pilot" have it all wrong! God does not need your help. He does not want to be your co-pilot. God is the only pilot. He wants you to give Him the wheel and trust that He will take you exactly where you need to go. God wants you to sit back and enjoy the ride!

Worry insults God. *"Now if God so clothes the grass in the field, which today is, and tomorrow is thrown into the oven, will He not much more clothe you, O you of little faith?"* (Matt. 6:30 NKJV). Worrying is like telling God that you don't think He can handle it. With every second we spend worrying, we are sending this message to God loud and clear: "I doubt You. I don't have any confidence in You. You're not big enough to take care of me." If you're a

Christian, then your lifestyle should include a lack of worry. Your friends and coworkers should see a peace in you that passes all understanding. You should have a peace because you know you are in God's hands. A person without God has reason to worry. They should worry about their needs, their provisions, their future, and where they will spend eternity. Those are legitimate concerns. But a person with Christ in their life has to learn to release their concerns and trust God. Looking around creates fear, but looking up releases faith.

No Worries

Have you ever heard the popular Jamaican song, "Don't Worry, Be Happy"? The words are so simple and right to the point, but they are exactly how God wants you to live your life! He doesn't want you stressing out and worrying about every little thing. You weren't created to worry about how you're going to make it or what's going to happen if things don't go right! You should be living a life without worries. Live with laughter and excitement! Be happy, just like the song says, because you're alive and God's looking out for you. He's not worrying about that situation you're going through, so why should you? He knows how it's going to turn out, so let Him be in control.

I was reading about J.C. Penney a few years ago in an article by Victor Parachin. Penny had several department stores around the country and business was going good. In the eyes of most people, he had it all. However, although things were going really well, he said he became completely overwhelmed with worry. He couldn't sleep at night and was getting sick. He started getting rashes and developed shingles. His doctor gave him a lot of medication, but none of the pills could help him shake the worry. He ended up going to bed one night convinced that he would die before morning. While he was lying in bed quivering, he heard a song playing. The words of the song were, "God will take care of you." J.C. Penney ran to the chapel that morning and knelt down and sang that song. Suddenly, he felt flooded with peace, like a dungeon door had opened and he had stepped into the sunlight. He said a miracle happened that day. He said, "For seventy-one years now, I can say, God took away all worry. It was the greatest moment of my whole life."

God wants to take away all of your worries as well. Stop focusing on your worries every day. Quit dwelling on things you can't control. Start believing God. *". . . [Y]our heavenly Father knows"* (Matt. 6:32). He's not surprised by anything that's happening in your life. He knows the end result, so relax and let God get behind the wheel of your life. Seek God first. *"But seek ye first the kingdom of God, . . . and all these things shall be added unto you"* (Matt. 6:33 KJV, emphasis added). Stop relying on your own resources and start relying on God when you're worried.

Turn your worries over to God. You'll be able to be at peace and fully enjoy life. Worry really is a waste of your time. It keeps you from trusting God. Start right now, saying,

"I'm not going to worry about my situation or problem any-more. I'm going to give it to God, because He's in control and He knows how this turns out." You'll feel the weights come off your chest if you do. Let God take care of your problems and don't let worry waste your life.

Chapter Seven

The Remedy for Rejection

What's Really Holding You Down?

We've all been there before . . . slightly swaying from side to side, popping our knuckles in a sort of pre-game stretch. As cold as it may have been on the playground, the kids could be even colder . . . Kickball day at recess—as the time came for the teams to be selected, you anxiously hoped that you would be one of the first chosen. Or at least not still standing on the sidelines as one by one, the line got smaller and smaller. You watch in agony as it dwindled down to five kids, and then four, three and . . . well, you get the point. No third-grader in their right mind wanted to get stuck in that situation, but we've all been there. What a cruel exercise to impose on impressionable young kids, who have yet to discover their true identity and self-worth! The entire class stands there with hopeful eyes, as two other students (who knows why they get to be the ones who get to pick which kid is better than the rest!) choose one by one who they deem worthy enough to be on *their* kickball team. Kickball. For many, this is where we get our first taste of rejection, and, trust me, it doesn't get any easier from here.

Truthfully, as I recall what it felt like to stand in front of my peers and hope to get chosen, I can't help but feel a twinge of anxiety. No one likes to feel judged, vulnerable, weak, or just plain not good enough! And this doesn't just apply to children—not many adults want to be in situations like this either! Who can blame us? Most people don't long to be in nerve-wracking situations that could lead to public rejection!

Rejection is the most powerful weapon one human can use against another. It is the root of a poor self-image, and a poor self-image stifles your potential for growth! Fear of rejection will keep you chained down and unable to become what God wants you to be. Fear of rejection will stunt your growth. There are some drugs out there that will stunt your growth if misused over a long period. Steroids, taken illegally by young people who have yet to hit their full physical maturity, can keep one from developing properly. Ever seen a young person who has some serious muscles in their upper body, but looks squatty because their body quit growing naturally? Their growth was stunted. That's what rejection does to people; it stunts their growth.

The scripture says, *"The fear of man brings a snare, but whoever trust in the LORD shall be safe"* (Prov. 29:25 NKJV).

Wow! Isn't that what rejection is really all about? Rejection is basically the fear of man. How many times do we end up avoiding certain situations altogether because of fear of what others might think? Or perhaps we go along with others because we don't want to be frowned upon or rejected. Maybe you don't voice your disagreement on an issue in front of a group of "friends" because you fear they might reject you. The same could be true whether it be around coworkers, strangers, or even family. Fear of rejection literally can trap you. That's what that word "snare" means in Proverbs 29:25, something that can trap you from being who God made you to be. Basing every decision on the rejection factor is no way to live. The important decisions you make in your life should be based on what the Bible says and how you feel God is leading you to decide. Important decisions cannot be based on what other people think!

A teenager who surrenders to peer pressure . . . a workaholic whose father told him he would never amount to anything . . . a wife who tolerates an abusive or lazy husband who doesn't provide for her . . . a person who constantly flatters people in order to be liked . . . a person who always is overbooked because he can't tell anyone no . . . a two-faced person who changes his personality depending on which crowd he is in . . . or a Christian who never speaks up for his church or tells anybody about Jesus. What do all these people have in common? Every one of them is driven by their fear of rejection!

If you really start to pay attention to the people around you, you will notice that people who have never known unconditional love usually are the easiest prey for rejection. Maybe you grew up in a broken home and your mom and dad weren't around. Or maybe you have never fully embraced the fact that God loves you. If you have never been in a relationship where you felt unconditional love, then you'll always be seeking it. Fear of rejection tricks us into thinking that we can fill the void in our life by going along with everybody else. If we agree with everyone, then more people will like us, right?

Rejection creates an emotional hole. It wreaks havoc on your self-esteem and causes you to question your self-worth. People with a fear of rejection work harder to get affirmation or acceptance, because they are looking outside of themselves for their value rather than to the One who placed it on the inside.

It is not uncommon for someone going through a divorce, or even a child of divorce, to battle rejection. A lot of times rejection is happening right at home . . . even in good homes. Have you ever heard someone compare one family member to another? Maybe it was not done intentionally to hurt someone, but it's just the same. You've heard it before: "Well, she's the smart one," or "He's the athlete in the family," or "She's the pretty one." These are all forms of rejection. Rejection, especially when it comes from family, wounds the soul.

It may seem funny, but adults face peer pressure just like teenagers. Oftentimes we associate peer pressure with those old "after school specials" on television. You know, the ones with the eggs and the frying pan. They were constantly reminding kids in high school not to fall into peer pressure. In reality, we never stop facing peer pressure, no matter how old we get. Directly or indirectly, you may have to choose whether or not to allow fear of rejection to inform your decision-making process in different situations in your life.

If you let the fear of rejection take hold of your life, you'll eventually find yourself living out someone else's life. Your goals will wind up sitting on the shelf if you let peer pressure dictate your choices. You'll end up throttling your potential. I knew a guy in college who was as smart as they come, but every semester he would not allow himself to make a 4.0. No matter what, he purposefully would squeak under with a grade point average of 3.9. One day I asked his father why his son had always come just shy of making a straight 4.0. I couldn't believe what he said! He told me, "John's afraid that if he does so well that he has a 4.0, then he would be considered a nerd. He doesn't want people to think he's a nerd, so he backs off to hide the fact that he's naturally smart." What a fear of rejection!

Fear of rejection will lead you to settle right into the life-style of those around you. It can play a factor in the clothes you wear, the car you drive, where you live, and how you think. It even can determine the very values you choose to adopt. God did not design you to have this fear. It will cause you to become a carbon copy of everybody else, instead of the unique and gifted person God called you to be. Fear invites people to manipulate you and prevents you from standing alone and speaking up.

Hear me clearly . . . Nothing, I mean *nothing* good comes from fear of rejection! It only creates loneliness, low self-worth, rebellion, and depression. Friend, don't let the fear of rejection step into your life and steal your joy. John 12:43 describes those people who believed in Jesus but wouldn't admit it for fear of the Pharisees: *"For they loved the approval of men rather than the approval of God."*

Fear of rejection will place you on the opposite side of God. Be bold and have courage under pressure. Don't be like those who were more concerned with the Pharisees' opinion of them than God's.

You Are Not Alone

It is so easy to feel like no one else understands you or really *knows* what you are going through. After all, no one is walking in your shoes but you, right? How can others possibly understand what you're feeling since they have their own problems to deal with? Sure, they may give you the obligatory hug, accompanied by those seemingly insightful, yet all too cliché, words, "Everything happens for a reason." But even with all of that, it's easy to conclude that other people just don't get it. And they probably don't . . . but Jesus does. Jesus gets it; He understands you perfectly! He gets every single thing you are going through. He totally, 100 percent understands you. He gets you.

Jesus was the most rejected person on earth; in fact, He still is today. We often overlook Jesus when we are battling rejection. We forget that the God and Creator of this universe experienced the same feelings of rejection that we do. Jesus' own hometown rejected him. They questioned His "supposed divine authority.". They thought, "Is this kid crazy? We all know who He is—He's Mary and Joseph's boy! He's the carpenter who grew up down the street; He's not anything special!"

Jesus offended people because of He associated with other outcasts. People rejected Him, saying, "Look at His friends—they're sinners!" Even His very own brothers and sisters found Him embarrassing. Jesus had all of the cards of rejection stacked against Him! His family, childhood friends, and entire hometown rejected Him! John 1:10-11 says, *"He was in the world, and the world was made through Him, and the world did not know Him. He came to His own, and those who were His own did not receive him."* Can you imagine? The very world He created rejected Him! The Jewish nation He was born into decided they didn't want anything to do with Him. Imagine what that felt like. Have you ever tried to do something nice for someone, only to be ridiculed by that very person? I know I have.

There used to be a man who walked ten to twenty miles, sometimes farther, just to get into town to buy groceries. I passed him walking down this particular rural road almost every day. One day I decided to stop. My wife and I pulled over and motioned for him to hop in the back of our truck. I thought I'd give him a ride into town. He didn't seem to understand, so I said, "Hey, man, I'd love to give you a ride into town! Why don't you hop in the back?" I thought he'd be thrilled with my gesture, but I was totally wrong! The guy was offended that I offered! He started yelling at me and Debbie, waving his hands hysterically in the air. It didn't take long for me to stomp the gas and get back on the road! Even though I was trying to help this guy out, he didn't like me one bit! I imagine Jesus must have felt the same way. When He looked down on His creation, He saw a world that desperately needed to be saved. He saw people He loved, who needed a Messiah. Jesus left His cozy spot in heaven to come to earth and take care of His people, but the people didn't want Him. He was rejected by those He came to redeem. Pretty unbelievable, isn't it?

Peter said in Acts 4:11 NKJV, *"This is the 'stone which was rejected by you builders, which has become the chief cornerstone'"* [emphasis mine]. And again in 1 Peter 2:4, it says, *"Coming to him as to a living stone, rejected indeed by men, but chosen by God and precious."* As was foretold by the prophet Isaiah, Jesus faced rejection throughout His lifetime. *"For he shall grow up before him as a tender plant, and as a root out of dry ground . . ."* (Is. 53:2). Jesus was a tender soul, but grew up in a hard society where people were mean and cruel.

Sometimes we don't realize how sinful and wicked people really can be. We are brought up in a sinful world, the effects of which can begin to tarnish our hearts at an early age. A schoolteacher approached me about a student in her class. This seven-year-old boy had lost his parents in a horrific fire. The teacher said that some of his classmates would put a cigarette lighter in his face to torment him. This young child, who had just lost his parents tragically, was being subjected to even more cruel pain . . . all because a group of older students thought that bullying him would help them be accepted by their peers.

More often than not, the root cause of rejection is actually acceptance. Isn't that ironic? Those who most want to feel accepted try to do so by rejecting others. It's a vicious cycle. I believe many of those young students really did not want to hurt their grieving classmate, but they valued their own acceptance over his. It was easier to fall in with the crowd than to show compassion and risk appearing weak in the eyes of others. No matter how tender you are, society can and often will mistreat you if you do not follow the crowd.

Maybe you grew up in a home where you did not feel like you were loved, and so you feel truly blessed to have made it as far as you have. You may feel like no one else understands what that is like, but Jesus does. Jesus knows what it is like to be misunderstood and rejected. Scripture goes on to say in Isaiah 53:2, *". . . He has no form or comeliness; and when we see Him, there is no beauty that we should desire Him."* Guys, this is telling us that Jesus was not the most beautiful person to ever walk the earth. He didn't look like Brad Pitt or George Clooney. Jesus' critics didn't like His earthly appearance because He didn't have exceptional physical beauty or look like royalty. To them, He looked too average and ordinary to be the Chosen One from God.

Isaiah 53:3 NKJV says, *"He is despised and rejected by men, a Man of sorrows and acquainted with grief. And we hid, as it were, our faces from Him; He was despised, and we did not esteem Him."* If you have ever felt like you were all alone in your rejection, think again. Jesus has been right where you are. Hated, falsely accused, criticized, and ridiculed by His own people. He knew these people better than they knew themselves. After all, He was their Maker. Yet, *He* was rejected by *them!*

If you have ever been rejected, Jesus knows exactly how you feel. He knows what it's like to be unfairly criticized, judged, slandered, and misunderstood. Let that be some divine encouragement for you. You're not alone when you are rejected. Even when you feel like there is not one person on earth who can understand how you feel, take heart that your Savior understands perfectly. Whenever you are rejected, friend, you are in good company! We are given that promise in Matthew 5:11-12: *"Blessed are you when people insult you and persecute you, and falsely say all kinds of evil against you because of Me. Rejoice and be glad, for your reward in heaven is great; for in the same way they persecuted the prophets who were before you."*

Rejoice in that truth! Many before and after you will battle rejection. Take refuge in that. Next time you're in a battle with rejection, look up and remember that you are not alone.

The Recall on Rejection

Attention! Attention! God has issued a recall from heaven. Anyone suffering from the fear of rejection is asked to hand it over to Him today. Don't waste another minute! Rejection can derail your life and force you to live in fear and captivity. If not relinquished, it promises to cause severe emotional distress!! Let go of it today!

Well it may not go quite like that, but I can promise you this: God would love to send out a universal recall on rejection. He would love to free you and me from its power. Most of us are going to face rejection at some point in our life, but we don't have to let it reign over us. You can choose to overcome rejection and not allow it to determine how you live your life. You can make a fresh start right now! Doesn't that sound great? It's as simple as doing these three things . . .

1. <u>Start placing God in His proper place.</u>

Psalm 27:1 says, *"The LORD is my light and my salvation; whom shall I fear?"* And later David says, *"For my father and mother have forsaken me, but the LORD will take me up"* (Ps. 27:10). If you know God loves you, then you can handle rejection. People often tell me that they wish they could learn to be more assertive so they wouldn't get run over. The secret to assertiveness is not getting psyched up, but believing that God loves you. When that sinks in, you'll be free of the snare of rejection. It will change the way you think. You will stop trying to please people at your own expense. Resting in God's love will allow you to decide that when others don't like you, it is their problem! The Creator and Lord of the universe loves you . . . just the way you are. God knows all of your flaws and insecurities; despite them all, He still looks at you as His child.

I love the fact that God looks at us differently. God does not see us the same way people do. It's as if He's looking at us through rose-colored glasses, but He sees us exactly as we are. Remember when God used Samuel to choose David by telling Samuel to look at the inside, not the outside. God looks at the heart. He doesn't care how much money you have, what kind of car you drive, or what level of education you have. People look at what you have, and then they accept you or reject you based on externals.

When Jesus came to earth, He didn't care what people had or didn't have. He didn't care how "religious" they were. Jesus inspected their hearts. The world doesn't view things the way God does. God sees our heart, what we're like on the inside. Do you truly know that God loves you? Do you believe it? If you do, then start living like it! Live your life knowing that the only person you need to please in the world is God the Father—no one else.

2. Place people in their proper place.

Now please don't misunderstand me here, I am not encouraging you to tell people off! Don't go let someone have it! Someone reading this right now is thinking, "That's all I need! I've got the pastor's permission to go tell John Doe off! I can't wait!" Don't do that. What I mean is for you to stop overvaluing the opinions and approval of others. You cannot please everybody. You need to accept the fact that not everybody is going to like you. It doesn't matter what you do. Some people aren't going to like you, regardless of how nice you are. Jesus knows this firsthand. So the first thing you have to accept is that some people are going to be unhappy with you no matter what. I love Isaiah 51:12. The Lord says, *"I, even I, am He who comforts you who are you that you are afraid of man who dies and of the son of man who is made like grass."* If popularity, applause, what people think, or your supposed image is important to you, you'll always be at the mercy of others. You don't have to live that way. Why should you value people's approval, when they are mortals, fading like the grass? The reality is people will never love you as much as you need. Human love is inconsistent and conditional. The scripture says it this way, *"For am I seeking the favor of men, or of God? Or am I striving to please men? If I were still trying to please men, I would not be a bond-servant of Christ"* (Gal. 1:10).

People may say some cruel things to you, but don't let it control your life. Sure it might hurt and affect you, but you don't have to let it direct you. Lloyd Oglilvie said, "Secure in God's love, I will not surrender my self worth to the opinions and judgments of others" (*Facing the Future Without Fear*, Oglilvie).

3. <u>Place yourself in your proper place in Christ.</u>

"In this is love, not that we loved God, but that He loved us and sent His Son to be the propitiation for our sins" (1 John 4:10). God doesn't love us for what we do but for who we are. God doesn't love you because you are valuable. You are valuable to God whether you make all A's or straight F's in school . . . whether you can cook the best meal in town or can't boil water . . . whether you have a degree in

astrophysics or are a kindergarten dropout. God doesn't love you because you are valuable. You are valuable because God loves you. You are so valuable that He sent His son to die on a cross for your sins so that you can have a relationship with Him.

Self-doubt is the reason we are so vulnerable to rejection. As soon as someone criticizes us, we start to doubt ourselves. We think there might be something *to* their negative comments. Self-doubting thoughts tell us, "Maybe I can't be successful, maybe I don't deserve any better." I want to encourage you not to listen to that voice; it's a snare. I am reminded of a friend in our church who was so afraid of rejection that he went several years without going on a date. This guy was in his forties and good-looking, but he was shy.

One day I was talking to him in the parking lot and asked him whom he was seeing. He told me he was not, so I asked him, "Is there anyone you are interested in?" He said there was and mentioned her name, but said he hadn't asked because he was afraid she might say no. That was all I needed to hear. I decided to make it my mission to get these two together. The next week after church, I grabbed my friend and said, "Look, I'll introduce you two to each other, and maybe you can ask her out after that." He was nervous, but agreed. So I introduced him to her. They were both pretty shy, so I did the talking for them. I told her that my friend would like to ask her out on a date. Of course, my buddy was turning red at this point, probably considering never speaking to me again, but then the lady looked right at him and said, "I'd love to. How about tomorrow night?" Stunned, he muttered, "That would be great."

Today they are happily married to each other. How awesome is that? And to think that if my friend would have let that fear of rejection continue to stand in the way of asking this woman on a date, he may never have met his wife. Put your faith in God. Don't worry about rejection; don't let it drive your life! Accept the fact that you are loved by God. The remedy for rejection is not rejecting the One who won't reject you.

Chapter 8

The Lure of Lust

There's More to It Than You Think!

A n old man had two dogs. These dogs were both very large and would fight with each other frequently. It seemed like the dogs never could get along. A young boy, who walked by the old man's yard every day and had noticed the dogs fighting, stopped by to chat with him. The boy asked the old man, "Which of the dogs usually wins?" The man replied, "Whichever one I feed the most."

When it comes to battling lust, I think a lot of us are similar to those two dogs. If we are feeding the desires of lust more than our spiritual life, then lust is going to win out every time. Lust is one of the most powerful emotions of all. As a Christian, you have a new nature that is constantly squaring off against your old nature. The only way to achieve victory is to starve that old nature. Jesus' half brother James describes the struggles of temptation and God's promise for those who overcome it:

> *Blessed is the man who endures temptation; for when he has been approved, he will receive the crown of life which the Lord has promised to those who love*

Him. Let no one say when he is tempted, "I am tempted by God"; for God cannot be tempted by evil, nor does He Himself tempt anyone. But each one is tempted when he is drawn away by his own desires and enticed. Then, when desire has conceived, it gives birth to sin; and sin, when it is full-grown, brings forth death. (James 1:12-15 NKJV)

Have you ever heard someone blame his temptation on God? Isn't that the easy way out? Just blame God for your struggles. The truth is that God cannot be tempted to do evil. No one can suggest to God that He give you something evil. Neither the devil nor any demon can suggest to God, "Why don't you do this to hurt your children?" God is holy and pure. He doesn't want to hurt you or keep blessings from you. Friend, God doesn't want to restrict you or see you fail. That's just not in His nature. God is immune and invincible to temptation; so don't worry about Him being tricked somehow by the devil to hurt His creation (James 1:13).

Another thing we need to understand is that God doesn't send temptation to us (James 1:13). If God sent temptation, then He would make Himself evil. Sure, God will allow us at times to be tested, but He gives us the power of choice and will always provide an escape if we need it. He may allow temptation, but He doesn't author it. God only allows it to prove that His grace is stronger. In fact, God says, "Be joyful" when you are tested, knowing that He will make a way for you (James 1:2).

Lust is one of the most effective weapons the devil has to use against you, because it is such a strong emotional desire. We often think lust is related only to sexual desire, but the truth is that lust doesn't have to be confined to sex. You can lust for many things. You can lust for fame, power, position, material things, money, a woman, or a man. You can even lust after gossip or revenge. You can lust for food. I deal with this whenever I walk by an ice cream shop. I'm lusting over the rocky road ice cream. And the list can go on and on. Lust is a craving to possess.

It doesn't matter who you are. From the church house to the White House, we see lust leading people to destruction. Think of the number of people in government alone who have been snagged by the lure of lust. It's everywhere and affects everyone . . . no one is exempt! But the secret is that you can overcome it if you are aware of it. You can conquer lust when you determine where you are most susceptible.

Everyone experiences lust. The scripture says *when* you are tempted, not *if* you are tempted (James 1:13). You are going to face temptation at some point in your life. Your temptation may not look the same as your neighbor's, but you will face it all the same. Don't think that being a Christian exempts you from lust or temptation. Actually, the more you try to live for God, the harder it will be. The more you elevate your life, the harder it is. There's an old, very true saying, "Greater levels bring greater devils."

One day a husband and wife were walking through the mall, when the husband spotted an attractive lady and turned all the way around to get a better look. His wife never batted an eye or looked back, but said, "I hope that was worth all the trouble you are in now." It doesn't matter how old we are or whom we're with, we are all going to deal with lust at some point. You get to choose whether you give in to it or not.

First Corinthians 10:13 says, *"No temptation has over-taken you but such as is common to man; and God is faithful, who will not allow you to be tempted beyond what you are able, but with the temptation will provide the way of escape also, so that you will be able to endure it."* Even when the temptations seem strong, you can call upon God to help you out, and He'll make a way.

What's So Enticing?

Fishing has some fundamental truths we can learn from, even if we don't enjoy the sport. Bass fishing is really an art. Essentially, you are trying to lure a fish through deception and trickery. There are a lot of similarities between bass fishing and temptation. The devil is trying to lure us away from growth in our faith. He wants you to fall flat on your face, so he constantly is changing his lures of temptation, in hopes that he will find something you can't resist. When the fish aren't biting a certain type of bait, you try another. The devil is throwing out all different kinds of lures to see which ones you'll bite.

He is a master angler, but he doesn't practice catch and release. The devil mounts his catches for the world to see. He has a trophy room full of preachers, deacons, worship leaders, business people, doctors, nurses, schoolteachers, and housewives. You name it and he's got it. He's caught someone in just about every profession. His lies have wrecked and destroyed numerous lives.

When you are going fishing, you study patterns; what time of day are the fish coming out and what is enticing them? Similarly, the devil studies patterns in our lives. Like fish, you and I are creatures of habit. Satan watches closely to see what interests we have and what our weaknesses are. Many fishermen use a tool called a depth finder to figure out where the fish are sitting. The devil uses his own depth finder to see where we really live. He knows not all of us live at the same level, with the same values. Some people live on the surface, some are deep in Bible and prayer, some have family values, and others have financial values. Whatever your own case may be, don't think he won't cast his reel in your direction to your exact depth.

The devil has a variety of lures. He knows he can't catch everyone using the same bait, so he makes sure that he brings his tackle box when he goes fishing. Three of his common lures of lust are similar to a fisherman's **buzz bait, worms, and deep divers.**

Buzz bait is a lure that comes across the water, looking attractive and making a lot of noise. This bait doesn't go unnoticed. It draws the attention of everything around it. The devil many times sends this bait in the form of a handsome guy at the office or the girl down the hall who looks like a fashion model. He sends that person who really turns heads and gets noticed. He hopes that if the buzz bait is dangled in front of you long enough, you'll take it. But like all bait, it has a hook underneath the flash and noise. Quite often, the devil uses another person to lure away a faithful spouse. In the Bible, Potipher's wife was the devil's buzz bait for Joseph. Watch out for the buzz bait; it's designed to deceive.

You also have to look out for **worms.** When you fish with a worm, it's slow and methodical. You want a worm to just brush by the fish slowly. I knew a lady, who, after breaking up her home as well as another, said she plotted for five years to go after her coworker. He left his wife to marry her, and now they both are struggling. She was like worm bait to him. Everyday she would brush by him, slowly trying to lure him in until he finally took the bait. In the Bible, Delilah did this to Sampson. She cleverly crafted her lure. Worm bait is not as in your face as buzz bait. It's subtler and takes time. Be careful that you don't start letting lust in your heart, or this bait can be used to pull you away slowly.

The third common lure the devil uses isn't for everyone. He uses the **deep diver** on those who are deeper in their faith. You throw a deep diver if you can't catch a fish with buzz bait or a worm. It swims several feet and then goes deep below the surface. The devil throws this out at those not easily swayed, who are little wiser and stronger in their faith. They read their Bibles and have a solid prayer life, so they aren't going to fall as easily. He has to work harder. He may not be able to get them with a charming coworker, but he can get them in other ways.

Remember, lust doesn't have to be just physical. You can lust after many things. The devil will study the patterns in your life to try and find a weakness. Make sure you are on guard and aware of the kind of bait he's pulling out of his box for you. Scripture says that everyone is lured by his own lust (James 1:14). Be the fish that got away!

The Fish That Got Away

When you're fishing, you know a fish is falling for your bait when you feel one slight tug on the line, followed by another. Sometimes you snatch your rod back, eager to see your catch, but nothing's there! It was close, but the fish resisted the bait and fled away to safety. When it comes to lust, I hope you'll be the one that got away. When temptation comes knocking at your door, don't linger in the foyer. Don't peer out the peephole and entertain the idea of letting it in. It's not that your life will be destroyed as soon as lust enters; the real danger is where lust leads. Think about it this way . . . **LSD**. Temptation starts with **L**ust, which gives birth to **S**in, which leads to **D**eath. Not just spiritual death, but also the death of all the good things in your life—your future, your potential, your family, your marriage, your finances, and everything in between.

When you see temptation coming your way, don't slow down and give it a glimpse; keep moving forward with your focus on God. I heard a funny story about a farmer who was worried about his chickens because of the traffic. The farmer lived right next to a busy street that was notorious for speeders. Concerned that someone might run over his chickens, the farmer called the sheriff. Unfortunately, the sheriff said that there was nothing he could do to make sure people slowed down. A few weeks later, after noticing slower traffic on the road, the sheriff stopped by to ask the farmer how he had solved the problem. The farmer replied, "I put a sign up that said, 'Drive slow. Nudist colony ahead.' Now they just creep by." You see, the farmer knew that temptation would get the best of them. Friend, don't creep by lust; keep driving with the pedal to the floor.

I was fishing in Eufaula, Alabama, a couple of years ago. It was mostly cloudy and cold, but I noticed the sun shining down brightly on this one little spot next to a rock. Now I'm not a great fisherman; but if I was a fish on that cold day, I'd be right next to that warm rock. So I threw my line in beside the rock, and within one minute I had caught a bass. I cast my rod six more times and caught six more bass. Stunned at how easy it had been, I thought, "You know, fish aren't too smart. You would think they would start getting a clue. I mean if I was Billy the bass hanging out with Charlie catfish and we started seeing our friends disappear one by one, I'd say to Charlie, "You know, every time one of our friends bites those baits, we never see them again." The ironic thing is that we are just like those clueless fish. Chasing bait to our own destruction. Splashing around, thrashing, being dragged away by the hook of lust.

I heard a man who had an affair once say, "My wife is dragging me into court." I don't think that was accurate. It was really his lust that dragged him there. There are three ways to avoid the lure of lust. The first thing is to flee. Just run away from temptation. If you are in a situation that you know you can't handle, then turn and go the other way. In the Bible, Paul told Timothy to *"flee youthful lust"* (2 Timothy 2:22). The longer you entertain, think about, or hang around temptation, the more likely you are to give in.

Secondly, you need to form beneficial relationships. Associate with people who are healthy and growing in their faith and life. Put people in your life who will keep you in check when you are getting off course. People who are destructive in their own life will only corrupt you.

Finally, to defeat lust, you have to focus. Saturate your soul in the Bible and aim your life at pleasing God. If your focus is on pleasing God, it's easier to say no to lust. How do you want your kids to remember you one day? Do you want to be remembered as someone who constantly struggled with temptation or someone who constantly overcame temptation? The choice is up to you.

If you win the little battles, you'll win the big one. There is an old Native American theory: "Each time a victim was scalped, the strength of that person was passed on to the one that did it." Every time you pass the test of life, you grow stronger. I want you to pass that test. Don't let the emotion of lust get you off track.

Chapter 9

The Hatchet of Hate

Hate Hurts

I'm not really sure what's worse, being hated on or being the hater. If you've ever been the object of someone's hate, you no doubt understand how miserable that can be. And if your heart ever has been consumed with hate for another person, you know what a toll it can take on your entire life. Hate hurts, no matter which side you're on.

Hate is a wicked emotion that blinds eyes to truth, steals peace, and ruins lives. Hate will destroy your life. That's exactly what it did to Joseph. His story is the perfect example of how hate can destroy the lives of everyone it touches, on both sides of the fence.

Genesis 37 begins the story of Joseph and his brothers. Joseph is a young boy with an innocent heart. He is a dreamer who loves God. His only crime is sharing his dreams with brothers he thinks he can trust. The problem is that in Joseph's dream his brothers one day bow down to him . . . not the kind of thing most older brothers want to hear! It also doesn't help Joseph's case that he happens to be his father's favorite son. Parental favoritism is a very dangerous thing for siblings, and in this instance, it makes Joseph's brothers burn with fury.

Let's take a look at the story found in Genesis 37:1-8.

Now Jacob lived in the land where his father had sojourned, in the land of Canaan. These are the records of the generations of Jacob. Joseph, when seventeen years of age, was pasturing the flock with his brothers while he was still a youth, along with the sons of Bilhah and the sons of Zilpah, his father's wives. And Joseph brought back a bad report about them to their father. Now Israel loved Joseph more than all his sons, because he was the son of his old age; and he made him a varicolored tunic. His brothers saw that their father loved him more than all his brothers; and so they hated him and could not speak to him on friendly terms. Then Joseph had a dream, and when he told it to his brothers, they hated him even more. He said to them, "Please listen to this dream which I have had; for behold, we were binding sheaves in the field, and lo, my sheaf rose up and also stood erect; and behold, your sheaves gathered around and bowed down to my sheaf." Then his brothers said to him, "Are you actually going to reign over us? Or are you really going to rule over us?" So they hated him even more for his dreams and his words.

The story goes on to tell us that Joseph's brothers are so overcome with hatred for their youngest sibling that they throw him into a pit and sell him into slavery. They take the beautiful coat Jacob had given young Joseph, cover it in goat's blood, and then bring it to their father as evidence that Joseph has been killed. Jacob mourns the "death" of his son and refuses to be comforted.

But obviously the story does not end there. Joseph becomes one of the greatest biblical examples of the hatred of men igniting the love of God. God never leaves Joseph's side during his seven years of slavery, servanthood, and imprisonment. God turns the situation around. Joseph definitely had suffered a traumatic life early on, but it has absolutely no effect on his destiny. God has a plan for Joseph even in the middle of his storms. In fact, Joseph goes on to become the second highest leader in the country. The key is that no matter how badly Joseph is hated on, *he* never allows hate to enter *his* heart. He even forgives his brothers personally many years later.

Joseph has a painful life when hate threatens to destroy him and keep him from the promises of God. But it is hard for his brothers, the haters, too. Often when we are the target of someone's hate, we think that we are the only ones hurting. It can be easy for us to think that the hater gets away with it, but that's simply not true. When we read between the lines of this story, we can see that Joseph's brothers don't get away with anything! Their life is hard and they are hurting, too! They have to live with the guilt of lying to their father about Joseph's death. Can you imagine watching a loved one suffer a broken heart because of a lie you fed him? I'm sure that took a toll on them.

We also see that the brothers begin to turn on each other. The Bible tells us that Reuben and Judah begin to argue with one another that they had done the wrong thing. One said to the other, "I tried to save him and you tried to kill him . . ." and so on (Genesis 37). All is not well within the family, and things certainly don't improve the way they had thought they would when Joseph is out of the picture. They become dysfunctional because of their hate.

A few years later, as if the guilt weren't enough, a famine causes the family to go bankrupt. They have to beg for food from the Egyptians, which is like begging your enemy to have mercy on you. They are forced to move as times got harder and harder. Obviously, the brothers do not get off free; their hate costs them hugely. It costs them their family bond, their comfort, their livelihood, and eventually, their pride.

Folks, I tell you this to give you comfort if you've ever been hated on. Now, don't delight in it, but know that when you are the victim of someone else's hate, that person will suffer as much, if not more, than you do. Joseph has God's grace on his life, while his brothers are hurting *without* the grace of God. Their consciences are bothering them, their finances are in a mess, and all seventy-five members of their family have to pick up and move in the days without the help of a U-Haul. Life is not easy for the haters.

God takes hate seriously. You may think that you are the only one hurting, but I can promise you that hate does the most damage to the one hating. The Bible tells us that God will not be mocked. It promises that whatever we sow, we also will reap. God takes it personally when His child is the object of hate; He will not be deceived.

The Ugly Truth About Hate

A wonderful member of our congregation recently made me a booklet of a bunch a memorable quotes he's heard me say over the years. Some of them are mine, others are from men much smarter than me. It was pretty interesting to look through all of those quotes and sayings . . . it made me realize that I am chock full of one-liners. My family calls them "Bill-isms." I have hundreds of these catch phrases that I use to help my congregation really remember the key point of my sermon. I think they're extremely helpful when memorizing an idea.

I've got a new one for you today. I made it up (not the idea, just the Bill-ism), but I think it wonderfully summarizes how God feels about hate and how easily hate can destroy your life and intercept blessings. Here you go . . .

A HEART THAT IS CONSUMED WITH HATE WILL CLOSE THE DOOR TO HEAVEN'S GATE.

If there is hate in your heart, there is no grace from heaven. If there's hate in your heart, there are no answered prayers. And most importantly, if there's hate in your heart . . . if hate consumes your heart, if it takes up *permanent* residence there, I don't think you can go to heaven. The Bible tells us that Jesus is meant to be the Lord of our heart and that Jesus is love. If Jesus is the contrast to hate, then hate cannot be of God. It's that simple. Your very life may depend on keeping hate out of your heart.

Nothing good happens in your life when hate takes over. Hate is in absolute contrast to God, and there is no good thing apart from God. Hate always finds a way to express itself outwardly, in the form of jealousy, criticism, gossip, slander, and much more. Hate looks for a way to vent, and when it does, it taints everything and everyone it touches. Let's take a look at what starts to happen in your life when hate takes over.

Proverbs 10:12 tells us that *"hatred stirs up strife."* Love covers, but hate provokes. Wherever you find strife, you'll find hatred at the root of it. People with hate in their heart actually get a kick out of causing conflict and trouble . . . they enjoy it! Have you ever been reminded of *The Jerry Springer Show* in someone's home? Everyone's fighting and arguing. It's mass chaos, but they love it. Have you ever known someone who seemed to delight in that kind of craziness? I have had people in my life who seem to hate me for no reason. I claim Matthew 5:11-12: *"Blessed are you when people insult you and persecute you, and falsely say all kinds of evil against you because of Me. Rejoice and be glad, for your reward in heaven is great . . ."* Some people hate me because they don't understand me.

Back in the early days of my ministry, I used to try to explain myself to everyone. I thought that if I explained who I was and why I was trying to go in a certain direction, then everyone who understood would get on the same page. I thought that I could dispel some of that hate . . . but I couldn't. I figured out quickly that if someone has made up his mind to hate you, there's not a whole lot you can do about it. I have had more dead-end conversations with people, thinking I could persuade and gain understanding with them, but for them, it was just a chance to argue. Once I tried to talk to a lady who was slandering me all over town, because I thought I could reason with her. I thought I could explain and help her see that what she was saying was wrong. Unfortunately, I found out quickly that she didn't want to reason with me, because she enjoyed arguing too much to let it go.

Don't waste your time on people like that: they just want to argue! I'm reminded of a statement Adrian Rogers made once. He said, "When you wrestle with a pig you both get dirty, but the pig enjoys it." Don't give pleasure to a pig! Proverbs 26:24 also warns us, *"He who hates disguises it with his lips, but he lays up deceit in his heart."* Now I'm not trying to teach you to be skeptical of everything and everyone, but this verse tells us to be careful about people who flatter you too quickly. My sons know this verse very well, and they really put it into practice because of the things they've witnessed as a pastor's kids over the years. All three of my boys are hard shells to crack. They love everyone and hope the best for everyone, but it can be difficult to make it to their closest circle of friends and people they trust. They don't let just anyone in.

About a year ago, my son Brent and I were in a meeting with a sharp group of businessmen. The leader of the group talked the talk and walked the walk. He was trying to sell us on some products and services, basically doing all he could to win our business. But when the meeting was over, this guy came over to Brent and reached out to hug him, saying, "I love you, brother." And Brent, being bottom line, put his hand up to stop him. He said, "You don't love me, you don't even know me," then stuck his hand out to shake the gentleman's hand. Brent finished, "Why don't we build a friendship first?" If that's not being real and authentic, I don't know what is.

Be leery of people who bring you into their inner circle too quickly, be discerning. Don't try to build instant friendships with everyone you meet. Watch out for people who say all kinds of flattering things to you without really knowing who you are or what you're about. I've always found that the relationships that sprout up overnight are like weeds. They come on quickly, but lack of foundation can cause them to be uprooted easily. Build your relationships over time and let them grow at a natural pace. You are going to build some of the best relationships when you go through valleys together. In the end, you will find that those seasoned relationships can be most trusted to stand the test of time. God will honor those kinds of friendships and will bless both parties. He will not bless relationships that are false and built on deceit, because God cannot bless hate.

The good news is that hate can be overcome, but it cannot be overcome alone. I don't think there's a ten-step program to overcoming hate or a secret truth that will dispel it from your life. I believe there is only one way to rid your life of hate: God's love has to fill your soul. One way or another, your heart will be filled with something. It is either filled with love or hate. You cannot simply say to yourself, "Well, I'm going to stop hating her so much starting . . . now!" It doesn't work like that. You have to take the hate out of your heart and fill that empty space with something else . . . the love of God. Romans 5:5 is a great verse: *". . . [T]he love of God has been poured out within our hearts through the Holy Spirit."* When the Holy Spirit pours His love in your heart, He will help you not to hate.

A pastor in Atlanta, Georgia, recently preached a series of sermons that caught the attention of the national media. The series was called, "We're Sorry . . . Really," and it focused on apologizing as a church and Christians to people and groups that we have been hateful toward in the past. The pastor, Dr. Richard Lee, told me he realized that we, as a community of Christians, owe an apology to people abroad that don't go to church. He said that, although he opposes abortion and believes that homosexuality is not a lifestyle approved by God, he still felt many Christians have condemned those people too harshly. He said that we have not acted lovingly toward those groups, even being cruel in many ways. While abortion and homosexuality are sins, many people have condemned rather than representing Christianity well by loving those people to Christ. Dr. Lee's series, "We're Sorry . . .

Really," was based on the idea that we as Christians not only owe some groups an apology, but also need to come up with a better strategy for reaching lost people. It's about love, not hate.

This church sparked national media attention because they were preaching love. It made a splash because it's not often that you hear about Christians doing anything other than letting everyone know what they're against. Telling the world you condemn them or hate them will take you nowhere. The world is eager to hear that Christians love them! You don't have to water down your beliefs in order to love people; you only have to learn how to speak the truth in love.

I don't think we always recognize hate in our own life, especially when we equate it with religious belief. God doesn't want us to hate anyone for any reason, especially not in the name of Him. The evidence of a Christian is love, never hate. First John 2:9 says, *"The one who says he is in the Light and yet hates his brother is in the darkness . . ."* No one will enter heaven's gate with a heart controlled by hate. If there is hate in your heart, I have to question whether or not you're really a Christian. The Bible makes it sound like that's not possible.

"But the one who hates his brother is <u>in the darkness</u> and walks in darkness, and does not know where he is going because the darkness has <u>blinded</u> his eyes."

—1 John 2:11

"Beloved, let us love one another, for love is from God; and everyone who loves is born of God and knows God. <u>The one who does not love does not know God, for God is love.</u>"

—1 John 4:7-8 (emphasis added)

"If someone says, "I love God," and hates his brother, he is a liar; <u>for the one who does not love his brother whom he has seen, cannot love God whom he has not seen.</u>"

—1 John 4:20 (emphasis added)

"By this all men shall know that you are My disciples, if you have love for one another."

—John 13:35

The only way to get hate out of your heart is to replace it with God's love. God's love has saved us from our sin and is the solution to every problem you will face in life. Take heart in this passage from the book of Titus: *"For we also once were foolish ourselves, disobedient, deceived, enslaved to various lusts and pleasures, spending our life in malice and envy, hateful, hating another. But when the kindness of God our Savior and His love for mankind appeared, He saved us . . ."* (Titus 3:3-5). God's love is the solution! His love can remove any trace of hate that ever takes root in your heart. It can wipe your slate clean.

That's what God's all about, you know? Making you clean, wiping the slate, new beginnings, fresh vessels, and so much more! Jesus came to the cross to deliver you from your sins. You are a new person once you put your trust in the One who came to create new life! Jesus came to save you from your sin. The wounds you have in this life, the scars of the past, and the failures you have faced can be healed through the love of God. The gifts you've been given are expressions of God's love for you. Use your life for His glory! Don't let the hatchet of hate cut a gaping hole in your life. Replace the hate in your heart with God's love and experience life like never before. Find the joy and peace that comes from loving others and being loved by the God of the universe.

Chapter 10

The Life of Love

Fight Fire With Fire

Natural disasters are a part of life on this planet. From tsunamis to tornadoes, earthquakes to floods, no matter where you live you are bound to encounter a natural disaster at some point in your life. Many of these natural disasters even have their own season, and I can appreciate that. At least when we are aware of the possibility of natural disasters, we can better prepare to handle them if they occur. We have hurricane season, the rainy season, severe-weather season, and many more. People who live in the parts of the world that endure those seasons do what they can to make the right preparations. They board up their windows, fill sandbags, and stock up on necessities like water and batteries. They know that if a hurricane hits, they may not be able to stop it; but they can do their best to get their property ready to combat it.

However, there is one natural disaster that actually can be stopped; it can be fought off. Yes, it can be very difficult and time-consuming, but men and women actually have the ability to stop this natural disaster. I'm referring to wildfire season. In many parts of the United States of America, there is a time of year known as fire season. The air and land are so dry and the winds are so strong that fires break out and become very difficult to control and extinguish. Fire season can vary among different geographical locations, depending on the season and climate. Florida, Texas, Wyoming, and California are most famous for their fire seasons, but wildfires are not exclusive to these states. Last year there was even a terrible wildfire on the coast of South Carolina . . . I guess it can happen anywhere!

Like many natural disasters, fires are a very scary reality that threatens the livelihood of hundreds of thousands of people. Wildfires often pop up quickly, without warning. Within a matter of minutes, thousands of acres of forests, fields, and even neighborhoods can get scorched to the ground. Because the wind and dry land help them spread quickly and erratically, wildfires leave a charred path of destruction and chaos. But they can be stopped.

We've all seen the airplanes and choppers on television that fly over the fires dropping water, right? Honestly, to me it looks like that water isn't even a drop in the bucket and cannot possibly be doing any good, especially in comparison to the vast flames below. But that's one way we are able to fight off wildfires.

However, there's another way that often works much better than dropping water out of the sky. It may sound crazy, but this method can snuff out even the most ferocious fires: fight fire with fire. I'm sure you've heard that expression before, but did you know that it is a legitimate defense mechanism? When you fight fire with fire, you actually are starting a controlled fire near the fire that is blazing out of control. You start the fire and let it burn for a little while, then put it out. This creates a firebreak, which is a strip of already burnt land. As the out-of-control wildfire approaches the firebreak, there is nothing for it to burn and consume, so it simply dies off. Thus, you have fought fire with fire.

Throughout this journey, we have learned that there is a way to overcome and defeat every negative emotion that can take root in our lives. We marched through the Bible and picked up valuable lessons along the way from people like David, Naomi, Joseph, Jesus, and many others. Their lives model not only the negative toll emotions can take on us, but also how we can make it out on the other side. Learning the disciplines of prayer, seeking and granting forgiveness, having faith, and finding contentment are just some of the ways to combat negative emotions . . . but there is one other way. We can fight fire with fire.

What better way to fight off negative emotions that become strongholds in our lives than with the most powerful emotion of all: love! Fight fire with fire. Fight your emotions with an emotion. Fight jealousy with love. Fight anger with love. Fight worry with love. Fight fear with love. Love is the most powerful emotion on earth. God created us out of love, He sent His Son to die for us out of love, and He redeemed us through love. Christ's love for us nailed him to a cross to die for our sins, and it is through that death that we gain life. Love defeated death; love can conquer all. Love can defeat your emotions. First Peter 4:8 NIV tells us, *"Above all, love each other deeply, because love covers over a multitude of sins."* Love will turn the tide in your life and enable you to start living the way God wants you to live . . . no longer defeated, but in victory!

Did you know that you are commanded to live a life of love? Love isn't just one option in the buffet line of life; it's *the* option that will keep you feeling full but always wanting to come back for more! Love is the answer! Jesus expects Christians to be people who love. He commands it in John 13:34-35, *"A new commandment I give to you, that you love one another, even as I have loved you, that you also love one another. By this all men will know that you are My disciples,* *if you have <u>love</u> for one another"* (emphasis added). It's amazing when you discover the simple power loving others will bring into your life. When you begin to live your life loving other people, as well as loving yourself, it's easier to keep from getting caught up in the negative emotions that try to sneak in.

Most Christians are familiar with 1 Corinthians 13, in which Paul eloquently describes love. This passage has been used in over half of the hundreds of weddings I have officiated over the years; it's not hard to see why. This one passage of Scripture beautifully paints the picture of all that true love has been, is, and will be. Although many believe the love Paul speaks of is romantic love between man and woman, I think we can divulge even more from this sweet scripture if we broaden our thinking to include not only romantic, but brotherly agape love as well. Please take a minute to read through this passage with me. Keep in mind the selfless, Christian love we are commanded to feel toward our fellow human beings.

Love is patient, love is kind.
It does not envy, it does not boast, it is not proud.

It does not dishonor others, it is not self-seeking, it is not easily angered, it keeps no record of wrongs.

Love does not delight in evil but rejoices with the truth.

It always protects, always trusts, always hopes, always perseveres.

— 1 Corinthians 13:4-7 NIV

Friend, don't miss the mountain of truth that is found in what you just read. Love is the purest emotion on earth and can be used to conquer every negative emotion you will ever face! Every emotion we've studied together can be cured with a dose of love. No, it won't always be quick and easy, but if you commit to combat your negative emotional strongholds with pure agape love, love will win out every time! Do you believe me? Better yet, do you believe what the Word of God tells you? It's all right there in that familiar passage, but you want me to prove it, don't you? I thought you'd never ask! Let's take a look at this passage line-by-line and discover the promises it offers us when we make love the goal of our life.

"Love is patient, love is kind."

I want to you to think about the most kind and patient person you know. It may be a parent, a sibling, or a friend, but think about the person in your life who most exhibits kindness and patience. What are they like? What kinds of qualities do they possess? When I think of that patient, kind person in my life, attributes like loving, compassionate, slow to anger, gracious, and diplomatic come to mind. I *don't,* however, see emotions like jealousy, bitterness, hate, and anger. When a person truly decides to live a life characterized by love above all other things, kindness and patience come to the forefront of that person's character, not negative emotions.

"It does not envy, it does not boast, it is not proud."

This one isn't too hard to figure out . . . love does not envy. In other words, love is not jealous! When you decide to truly love everyone around you, you will find it very difficult ever to be jealous of those people. I love my wife. I mean I really, really love my wife. And I love my boys. Jealousy is not something I've ever really struggled with, but I can promise you this: I've never been jealous of my wife or my kids. I've never seen them be blessed and thought,

"Man, that's not fair! I want what they have!" Never. Why? Because you are not jealous of those you truly love. It's not possible! Love will win the battle over jealousy every day of the week and twice on Sunday!

"It does not dishonor others, it is not self-seeking."

Love is not rude or self-seeking. When a person is filled with love and their number one goal is to exemplify that love to others, others' desires and needs become the most important thing. When you put the desires of others above your own, you will never fall into the temptation of lust. Lust is an emotional desire that does not fall within proper parameters; it's a desire that's out of check. It's possible to lust for many things: fame, attention, power, the opposite sex, a position, and much more. However, when you are not living a self-seeking lifestyle, it is impossible to succumb to the temptation of lust. A self-seeking person only cares about themselves and doesn't give much though to other people. But an "others-seeking" person puts the needs of others before his own. Lust is selfish, love is selfless.

". . . [I]t is not easily angered."

My daughter-in-law is absolutely crazy about her little dog, Sophie. She and my son don't have any children yet, so this dog is like their child. What's hilarious is that this little four-pound Maltese can be a real terror. She's a fluff-ball of fury! Sophie is very aggressive toward strangers and other dogs. She barks and barks like a maniac, and nothing can snap her out of it! Last Christmas, my mother-in-law was visiting and met little Sophie for the first time. Sophie did not like Mee-Maw (that's what my boys call her). Every time Mee-Maw entered the room, Sophie would try to chase her out of it. She even caught Mee-Maw's house robe in her teeth and started playing tug of war with it! The dog has problems! But my daughter-in-law loves her dog. She's her baby, and Sophie's nutty behavior never seems to anger her! Sophie is the first dog she's had that she can really call her own, and she loves her.

Love is not easily angered. When you turn the dial up on love, you're automatically turning the dial down on anger. Of course, we all have a right to get angry when it is justified, so please don't misunderstand me. But becoming easily angered . . . that's for the birds! Who wants to spend their life getting angry at every little thing? You won't when you live a life of love!

". . . [I]t keeps no record of wrongs."

There are two negative emotions that come to my mind when I read this short phrase . . . bitterness and guilt. Isn't that what both of those emotions are all about? Bitterness is when we hold on to a past hurt and let it eat away at our joy, and guilt is often when we take the blame for something, justified or not, and let it steal our peace. Either way, bitterness and guilt sneak into our lives when we keep a record of the wrongs done to us and by us.

A life of love is not like that. True love does not hold on to past hurts and failures, but lets them go. When you let love guide your life and your relationships, you learn to forgive and let go. Colossians 3:13-15 NIV reminds us,

Bear with each other and forgive one another if any of you has a grievance against someone. Forgive as the Lord forgave you. And over all these virtues put on love, which binds them all together in perfect unity. Let the peace of Christ rule in your hearts, since as members of one body you were called to peace. And be thankful.

When you put on the virtue of love, it brings unity into your life. Bitterness and guilt fall by the wayside when love is at the center. Love forgives, love forgets, and love unites.

"Love does not delight in evil but rejoices with the truth."

This one-liner puts to death the emotions of hate and rejection. It squashes them, and they are no more. Hate is evil, pure and simple. As Christians, we are called to a life of love. There's no room for hate in a believer's heart. Hatred is evil. Hate pushes people toward evil like gossip, slander, and even murder. Love is the cure for hate. When love is the goal, hate cannot survive. Love and hate cannot co-exist in the same heart; when one moves in, the other moves out.

Love also rejoices with the truth, which takes care of your fear of rejection. Love cares only about what it true, and what is true is that God created you and loves you more than you will ever fully grasp. Rejection causes you to worry about what other people think of you, instead of believing the truth of what God says about you. Other people may say that you are worthless, but God says you are worth dying for. Other people may say you are unlikable, but God says you are loved beyond measure. Love rejoices in the truth and throws out any hint of falsehood. When you rejoice in the truth of God's unending love for you, the fear of rejection from no man can take root.

"It always protects, always trusts, always hopes, always perseveres."

Love protects, so what is there to fear? Love trusts, so what can make you worry? When your life is 100 percent about loving God and loving others, then you have nothing in the world to fear. Love protects. *"Whoever loves their brother and sister lives in the light, and there is nothing in them to make them stumble"* (1 John 2:10 NIV). God instructs us to love our brothers and sisters in Christ and promises us that when we do, nothing will be able to make us stumble. We will have nothing to fear!

Love also basks in a spirit of trust. Love trusts God. Love trusts the good in people. Love knows that with God on the throne, there is nothing to worry about! Love trusts the promises of God.

Love can cure the most jealous, angry, bitter, guilty, fearful, lustful, worrying, hateful, rejected person on the planet! I know it sounds cliché, but love truly *is* the answer. You are commanded to live a life of love! You are promised victory when love is your battle cry! Love is the most important and powerful emotion of all time. It makes the impossible possible, brings healing to the sick, pours life into the lifeless, and opens up freedom to those in bondage. Love is evidence of God's heart for us. When you make loving a priority, it glorifies your Savior, Jesus Christ. First John 4:7 ensures us that our love for others proves our love for God. It says, "*. . . [L]et us love one another, for love is from God; and everyone who loves is born of God and knows God.*"

Emotions are fluid, and they will come and go in your life. I sit here knowing that all of us, myself included, will battle our emotions from time to time. Don't let your emotions cause you to make bad decisions and derail your life from the plan God has for you. Fight fire with fire! Fight your negative emotions with love! Live a life that embodies all that love is. Make a decision to let love, and love only, prevail. You can't go wrong when pure, selfless, agape love is at the center of your life.

The disciple John, James's brother and Peter's best friend, really understood Jesus' message about love. He is the one who, after all, penned himself as "the disciple whom Jesus loved" (John 13:23). John understood the power that comes when we place ourselves in the center of God's love. Through John's gospel, Jesus urges us to remember to dwell in His love. He says to us in John 15:9 NIV, *"As the Father has loved me, so have I loved you. Now remain in my love."* In the New King James Version, the word "remain" is replaced with the word "abide."

Jesus invites us to remain, to abide, in His love. He wants us to park our car in the middle of His love and stay there. He invites us to dwell in the power and assurance of His love for us. Jesus' love isn't a fast food drive-thru window. He doesn't want us to fly through when we're in a hurry and need a quick pick-me-up. Instead, He invites us to stop and stay awhile. Jesus wants us to take off our jacket and get comfortable, so comfortable, in fact, that we never want to leave. Remain in His love. Dwell in His love. Abide in His love.

So go ahead, kick off your shoes. Put on your coziest pajamas. Let the God of the universe wrap His loving arms around you and demonstrate the life-changing power of His love. But a word of warning . . . you better get ready to stay a while. Once you experience the comfort and peace that comes from the love of Christ, you'll never leave again.

"If you always do what you've always done, you'll always be where you've always been." -Dr. Bill Purvis (1974)

Bill Purvis Leadership is a monthly mentoring program for those unique people with a serious passion to grow and reach their goals in life. Life gives us honest feedback based on our efforts, choices and strategies of the past. A better life and better results are possible, but most people won't make the effort to improve. They would rather make excuses, complain about their situation, or envy those living the life they want.

By implementing the Biblical truths contained in each Bill Purvis Leadership lesson, you will experience growth on a personal, professional and spiritual level that only God could have planned. Begin the journey to reaching your full potential today.

Professional Mentoring Package	Advanced Leadership Mentoring Package	Executive Mentoring Package	
Streaming Audio Access to the latest (3) streaming audio messages. **Downloadable PDF Notes** Follow along with printable PDF note sheets. **Weekly E-Devotionals** Get weekly devotions direct to your inbox.	**New Leadership Lessons** Receive a fresh new leadership lesson each month on CD and/or audio streaming. **Streaming Audio** All access to archived leadership audio messages. **Streaming Video** Bi-monthly leadership video tips. **Downloadable PDF Notes** Follow along with printable PDF note sheets.	**Leadership Blog** Access to Dr. Purvis' leadership blog/ occasional video blogs. **Weekly E-Devotionals** Get weekly devotions direct to your inbox. **Interviews** Access to leadership interviews with other outstanding leaders. **Leadership Tips** Receive bi-monthly leadership tips directly to you inbox.	**All Features Plus:** Current 4-Part sermon series mailed to your home or office monthly!

Pray for Your Pastor

Bill Purvis is living proof that God answers prayer! Having been stabbed three times with a butcher knife and left for dead at the age of 18, God answered his prayer for salvation and spared his life from imminent death. Since that day he's been passionate for God and devoted to the practice of prayer.

So many times we imagine that our pastors lead picture-perfect lives...that things always go their way, nothing bad ever happens, and most importantly, that there is nothing they could ever need from us. That couldn't be further from the truth! Hear first-hand the truth behind the stained-glass and come to a greater understanding of why your pastor needs your prayers.

For additional resources from Dr. Purvis please visit us at www.billpurvis.com